Power Tennis Training

Donald A. Chu, PhD
Ather Sports Injury Clinic
Castro Valley, California

Human Kinetics

Library of Congress Cataloging-in-Publication Data

Chu, Donald A. (Donald Allen), 1940-
    Power tennis training / Donald A. Chu.
        p.   cm.
    Includes index.
    ISBN 0-87322-616-X
    1. Tennis--Training.   2. Physical education and training.
    3. Exercise.   I. Title.
    GV1002.9.T7C48   1995
    796.342'07--dc20   94-21325
                                                                                    CIP
ISBN: 0-87322-616-X

Developmental Editor: Rodd Whelpley
Assistant Editors: Hank Woolsey, Ann Greenseth, and Jacqueline Blakley
Copyeditor: Kenneth Walker
Proofreader: Sue Fetters
Typesetter and Layout Artist: Kathy Boudreau-Fuoss
Text Designer: Stuart Cartwright
Cover Designer: Jack Davis
Photographer (cover): Michael Baz
Illustrator: Paul To
Printer: United Graphics

Human Kinetics books are available at special discounts for bulk purchase. Special editions or book excerpts can also be created to specification. For details, contact the Special Sales Manager at Human Kinetics.

Printed in the United States of America

10 9 8 7 6 5 4 3 2 1

Human Kinetics
P.O. Box 5076, Champaign, IL 61825-5076
1-800-747-4457

Canada: Human Kinetics, Box 24040, Windsor, ON N8Y 4Y9
1-800-465-7301 (in Canada only)

Europe: Human Kinetics, P.O. Box IW14, Leeds LS16 6TR, England
(44) 532 781708

Australia: Human Kinetics, 2 Ingrid Street, Clapham 5062, South Australia
(08) 371 3755

New Zealand: Human Kinetics, P.O. Box 105-231, Auckland 1
(09) 309 2259

CONTENTS

Foreword   **vii**

Introduction: What Is Power Tennis Training?   **1**

The Power Tennis Training Conditioning Program   3
The Components of Power Tennis Training   4
How to Use This Book   6

Part I   Power Tennis Training Components   7

Chapter 1   Exercise Principles for Tennis Players   9

Exercises Needed for Power Tennis   9
Planning Effective Workouts   10

Chapter 2   Warm-Up and Stretching Exercises   15

Warm-Up Exercises   16
  Side Lateral Raise   18
  Front Raise   20
  External/Internal Rotation (Faceup)   21
  Prone Fly   22
  Arm Circles   23
Stretching Movements   24
  Shoulder Stretch 1   25
  Shoulder Stretch 2   26
  Wrist/Forearm Stretch   27
  Postworkout Stretches   28

Chapter 3   Weight Training and Trunk Exercises   33

General Performance Guidelines: Free Weights   33
General Performance Guidelines: Machines   34
Weight Training Exercises   35
  Back Extension   36
  Back Squat   38

Bench Press   40
Bench Step-Up   42
Calf Raise (Machine)   44
Calf Raise (Seated)   46
Cross-Over Lunge   47
Dumbbell Row   48
Dumbbell Split Jerk   49
External Shoulder Rotation (On Side)   50
External Shoulder Rotation (Seated)   52
45-Degree Lunge   53
Front and Back Pulldown   54
Front Lunge   56
Front Squat to Push Press   57
Glute-Ham Raise   60
Incline Press (Barbell)   62
Leg Curl (Facedown)   64
Leg Press   66
Pec Dec   68
Pullover   70
Pullover and Press   72
Push Press   73
Seated Row   74
Side Lunge   76
Upright Row   78
Walking Lunge   80
Wrist Flexion/Extension   81
Wrist Pronation/Supination   82
Wrist Ulnar/Radial Flexion   83
Trunk Exercises   84
Bicycle   85
Hip Press-Up   86
Hip Roll   88
Hip Rotation   89
Knee Pull-In   90
Russian Twist   92
Side Sit-Up   94
Sit-Up With Legs Raised   96

Chapter 4   Plyometric and Medicine Ball Exercises   97

Plyometric Exercises   97
Depth Jump With Lateral Movement   98
Hexagon Drill   99
Jump and Reach   100

Jump Over Barrier (Side)   101
Jump to Box   102
Lateral Cone Hops   103
Push-Up With Clap   104
Side-to-Side Box Shuffle   105
Single Leg Push-Off   106
Split Squat Jump   107
30-60-90 Box Drill   108
Medicine Ball Exercises   109
Bench Step-Up and Press   110
Drop Pass   111
Kneeling Side Throw   112
Overhead Throw   113
Pullover Toss   114

Chapter 5   Court Drills

115

The Court Drills   116
Court Drill 1   118
Court Drill 2   119
Court Drill 3   120
Court Drill 4   121
Court Drill 5   122
Court Drill 6   123
Court Drill 7   124
Court Drill 8   125
Court Drill 9   126
Court Drill 10   127

Part II   Power Tennis Workouts

129

Chapter 6   Building Blocks Approach to Workouts   131

Chapter 7   Block 1: Strength-Endurance Workouts   133

Chapter 8   Block 2: Strength Workouts   141

Chapter 9   Block 3: Power Workouts   149

Appendix   Fitness Testing Worksheet   157

Exercise Index   161

About the Author   165

FOREWORD

For the past 10 months I have participated in Don Chu's Power Tennis Training program. During this time I have come to know Don and to understand more about physical fitness, tennis, and myself.

The United States Tennis Association referred me to Don Chu in 1992 shortly after the U.S. Open. The USTA player development coaches, Stan Smith, Tom Gullikson, and Jose Higueras, recognized that I needed to improve my agility, stamina, strength, and power. As I was somewhat injury-prone, they determined that Dr. Chu's program was not only well suited to my fitness and strength goals, but also structured to help me avoid future injury. So in November I arrived at Don's Castro Valley clinic to begin the Power Tennis Training program.

We began with a series of strength, quickness, and flexibility tests. Don then took me step-by-step through weight lifting, plyometric, and stretching procedures, followed by on-court drills. Even though I had worked on these things before, the structure of Don's workouts was innovative, making them both interesting and effective. Specifically, Don and I worked in circuits, alternating strength and power exercises. In a typical circuit I would do 12 bench press repetitions followed by 12 medicine ball throws, and then repeat the circuit. An added bonus to Don's program was that I could do the workouts alone. After a week I hit the road, and the gym, on my own.

I had 2 months to train hard before the tournament season resumed. Don's workout blocks provided an excellent supplement to my tennis training. With periodic phone calls to Don I improved my technique and strength in the gym. After those 2 months I was fitter than ever before. I felt protected from injury, stronger, quicker, and, most of all, more powerful! Most important are the tremendous effects Power Tennis Training has had on my overall game!

Don Chu has hit the nail on the head. He has developed a program specific to tennis players that is safe, fun, and, most of all, extremely effective. His book, *Power Tennis Training*, will help any athlete strive for and achieve his or her physical potential.

—Todd Martin
August 1993

INTRODUCTION

WHAT IS POWER TENNIS TRAINING?

In the book *Ladies of the Court*, Michael Mewshaw suggests that an apparently inappropriate weight training program used by Gabriela Sabatini early in her career made Sabatini "much heavier and slower. Broad-shouldered and muscle-bound, she swaggered around the court looking, in the words of Teddy Tinling, like John Wayne—but a John Wayne who couldn't shoot straight and couldn't kill off the enemy."

In 1990, Sabatini teamed up with Carlos Kirmayr, a coach who "preached speed and quickness." Mewshaw says that "as he ran her through a regimen of jumps, lateral lunges, and sprints, Sabatini lost weight and gained agility. Her movement on court became more explosive, and so did her shots." Several additional factors were responsible for Sabatini's success, but this example emphasizes the idea that it's important to train not only hard but smart.

Athletes are learning that strength training helps prevent injuries and enhance performance, especially in light of increased power associated with today's game. Not only will strength training limit the number of injuries that occur, it will help players bounce back from their injuries faster.

My advice to you as a tennis player is to adopt a *balanced* approach to conditioning. Weight training is important, but it must be properly implemented so you don't develop large, bulky muscles that will slow you down and hamper your endurance. A balanced conditioning system for tennis requires a combination of training methods, and this is where the concept of *power* comes in.

Power is speed applied to strength. It's great to be strong, but the player who can hit the ball the hardest is the one who can apply that strength effectively. The graph in Figure 1 shows the results of two methods of training.

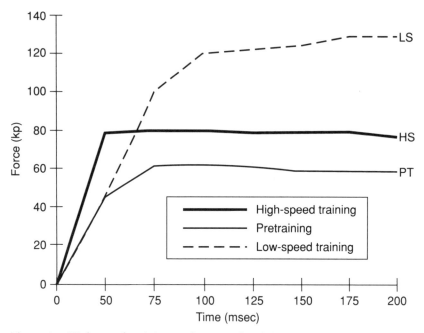

Figure 1. High-speed training vs. low-speed training.
Note. From "Five Steps to Increasing the Effectiveness of Your Strength Training Program" by C. Poliquin, 1988, *The National Strength and Conditioning Association Journal*, **10**(3), p. 38. Copyright 1988 by The National Strength and Conditioning Association. Reprinted by permission.

The dotted line represents the training of bodybuilders and powerlifters, athletes whose workouts emphasize lifting weight at slow speeds. These athletes can produce a great deal of force, but it takes them a relatively long time to display it. The thick line represents the type of high-speed training methods that are emphasized in *Power Tennis Training*. Although low-speed training equips athletes to generate more force, athletes who use high-speed training can reach their maximum strength level faster. And with the speed at which tennis is played, this means athletes who use the Power Tennis Training conditioning program will be faster and able to hit the ball harder.

● The Power Tennis Training Conditioning Program

As shown in Figure 2, the Power Tennis Training program consists of three blocks that emphasize strength and endurance, strength, and power. Part II of this book describes the daily workouts that make up each training block. You will perform the blocks in succession, each block taking 4 weeks to complete.

In the first block you're getting your body familiar with the exercise routine and developing strength in the muscles, tendons, and ligaments. This will prepare you for the more dynamic and heavier weight exercises later on. In the second and third blocks, you increase your intensity to maintain a progressive loading of the muscles. This in turn develops a greater ability to produce force without sacrificing speed. After 12 weeks you can begin again with Block 1. By that time you'll begin to notice that you are quicker and hitting the ball with more authority—and so will your opponents.

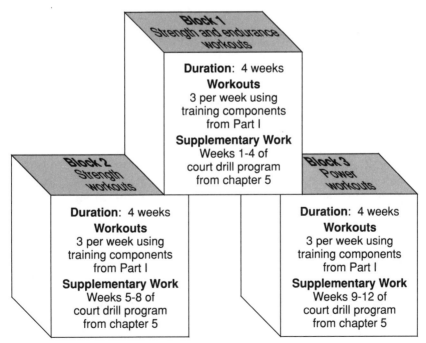

Figure 2. The three blocks of the Power Tennis Training program.

⬤ The Components of Power Tennis Training

Power Tennis Training combines a number of different training methods, including weight training, trunk exercises, plyometrics, medicine ball exercises, and court drills. Part I of this book details these methods and demonstrates the individual exercises that make up the workouts described in Part II.

Here is a brief overview of the program with comments on the overall conditioning and fitness testing, the injury prevention techniques, and the proper diet that necessarily accompany it.

Weight Training

A major element of the Power Tennis Training program is weight training. Because the lifts used in the program are multijoint exercises, you don't have to worry about getting big and bulky and slowing down in the process. In fact, the exercises in this program develop not only skill for lifting and strength building but are designed for the specific needs of tennis players. The weight training exercises transfer easily to the game.

Weight training is best performed before a tennis workout, when your body is fresh and still has ready stores of energy. Also, by doing these exercises first, you prepare your nervous system for the tennis that follows.

Trunk Exercises

Another element that you'll notice emphasized in this program is strengthening of abdominal muscles. Experience has taught me that the weakest area in many tennis players, even good ones, is the abdominal muscles. For this reason, I've included trunk exercises that stabilize the spine and protect you from injury. You need to be able to connect the upper and lower halves of the body to generate the tremendous torque necessary for hard serves and ground strokes. Solid abdominal muscles are essential to make this connection. In addition, building stronger abdominal muscles can improve your balance on court.

Plyometrics

Another component is plyometrics, a method of training that emphasizes high-speed movements. The physiology of plyometrics is covered in detail in my book *Jumping Into Plyometrics* (available through Human Kinetics), but it's important for you to understand that plyometrics trains you to apply speed to your strength. Plyometrics can help you accelerate faster, change directions more quickly, and give you a better first step on the court.

Medicine Ball Exercises

The weight training components of the program de-emphasize the use of weight machines and favor the use of free weights and medicine balls since these types of equipment allow you to develop the specific movement patterns needed for tennis. In contrast, an isolated joint exercise performed on a machine may be good for developing strength in that particular joint, but may not have any real bearing on functional strength for the game of tennis.

Court Drills

Since you want to keep training as tennis-specific as possible, you'll see that the program includes some on-court exercises as well. The on-court elements of this program are supplementary, and they're not intended to be all-encompassing as conditioning exercises. These exercises allow you and your coach to work on your running form and technique for change of direction. They let your coach examine your ability to sprint across court and shuffle laterally—running techniques that can be improved with practice.

Overall Conditioning and Fitness Testing

Although you won't see any prescriptions for aerobic conditioning in this program, an aerobic base is an important component of fitness for tennis. As a tennis player, you need to include some aerobic exercise, but this should not be your dominant conditioning exercise. *Power Tennis Training* includes an appendix with information about fitness tests, including tests for aerobic capacity. Pretraining fitness testing establishes a baseline for fitness and lets you set a goal to work toward—something to plan your program around. Improving the components of strength, speed, and fitness will mark the fact that your physiological abilities are improving.

Safety and Injury Prevention

As you're building strength and muscular balance, you can be sure you're helping to prevent injury. The program stresses that you prepare your muscles for work by prescribing a three-part warm-up before each workout. Every workout is followed by 5 to 10 minutes of postworkout stretches to prevent tightness. If you have back or knee problems, this program should not aggravate your condition. You may have to limit some of the plyometric activities, and if you have acute problems you may have to be careful how you do these activities or eliminate them completely. You should also perform them under the guidance of someone who is knowledgeable about injuries and strength training.

Proper Diet

This program also assumes you have the physical wherewithal to meet the demands of competition and training. That means eating right. While it is beyond the scope of this book to offer specific nutritional advice, you should be eating a diet that is around 64% carbohydrate, about 19% protein, and 17% fat. Most players will need an average daily intake of just over 1,800 kilocalories a day. If you haven't been paying attention to your eating habits, perhaps you should. Consult your trainer or a dietician or published resources such as *Nancy Clark's Sports Nutrition Guidebook* for expert advice. Remember, you can't race hard on the wrong fuel, so eat to train like a winner.

● How to Use This Book

There are two ways you can use this book. If you have an extensive background in conditioning methods, you can review the court drills in chapter 5 and then proceed to the workouts in Part II. With this approach, you'll be able to start the Power Tennis Training program after only a few minutes of reading. If you have concerns about how to perform any exercise in the program, simply refer to the appropriate chapter in Part I.

If your knowledge of conditioning methods is limited, you should read the book from start to finish. Whichever way you use the book, my video *Jumping Into Plyometrics* (available through Human Kinetics) will teach you how to perfect your technique on the more complex exercises I've prescribed in this program.

I hope you'll decide to give Power Tennis Training a try. I've made this program as practical as possible, but I didn't make it easy. Power Tennis Training is a serious program for the serious athlete. You may not always like the hard work, but you'll love the results.

TRAIN HARD!

POWER TENNIS
TRAINING
COMPONENTS

CHAPTER 1

EXERCISE PRINCIPLES FOR TENNIS PLAYERS

There are two basic types of physical workout programs: body-building programs that make you look great and sports-conditioning programs that make you play great. A person who bodybuilds may not necessarily want to pose in front of an audience but may simply want to lose a few pounds and look better. Although a body-building program will help prevent injuries, it is not the best way to condition a tennis player. Building bulky muscles in certain areas may actually slow you down and hinder your performance. I designed Power Tennis Training specifically to improve the athletic abilities needed to play better tennis. If it also makes you look better, consider that a bonus.

Exercises Needed for Power Tennis

Well-designed sports-conditioning programs involve performing activities that develop abilities specific to an athlete's sport. A tennis player needs to become stronger, faster, and more agile, and to improve endurance. When I was designing the Power Tennis Training workouts, I studied the movements that occurred on the tennis court and selected conditioning exercises that simulated those activities. I also selected exercises that would prevent injuries by correcting muscle imbalances, particularly in the shoulder area. So, for example, in this program you'll see exercises that work to balance your internal and external rotator muscles.

You're probably saying to yourself, "What's so special about tennis that I need a tennis-specific conditioning program?" The answer is that tennis involves an amazing number of muscle groups, each of which makes a specific contribution to performance of the required skills. Table 1.1 shows the various muscle groups involved and how each of them contributes. It also lists the exercises in this program that provide the specific training needed to enable each muscle group to perform its function effectively and safely. (Details of each exercise are given in chapters 2 through 4.)

Before I describe the exercises you'll be doing, let me give you some important general tips on planning effective workouts.

◉ Planning Effective Workouts

Part II prescribes the workouts that make up the three 4-week blocks of workouts of the entire Power Tennis Training program. You'll see that each workout is built from components described in Part I. You'll get more from your workouts if you understand some of the principles I used to design these workouts.

Number of Exercises

How many exercises should you perform in a workout? I believe there is a limited amount of time you can spend in the weight room and still perform quality work. Generally, more than 10 weight training exercises per workout is too much unless those exercises work smaller muscle groups.

Order of Exercises

How should you arrange your exercises in a workout? It's best to perform the more complex (multijoint) exercises first—when you're fresh—as these will make the most significant impact on your conditioning. Also, fatiguing the smaller muscle groups early in the workout will prevent you from generating maximum intensity on the bigger muscle groups. If, for example, you were to train your biceps with curls early in a workout, it would be difficult for you to perform heavy rows for your back muscles later in the workout. This is why I've put the complex portions of the daily workouts early in the workout.

Table 1.1 The Tennis-Specific Components of the Power Tennis Training Program

---

I • FOOT SPEED

In tennis you know the first thing you have to do is get to the ball. Most of the exercises in chapter 4 develop the quick foot speed you need to get to every ball. By reducing foot contact time, you'll cover the court more quickly and efficiently and get to balls you never dreamed possible. These plyometric exercises will make you a little stronger and a lot faster:

- Depth jump with lateral movement
- Hexagon drill
- Jump and reach
- Jump over barrier (side)
- Jump to box
- Lateral cone hops
- Push-up with clap
- Side-to-side box shuffle
- Single leg push-off
- Split squat jump
- 30-60-90 box drill

II • LOWER EXTREMITIES (LEGS)

Tennis power starts at ground level and works its way up through your body. By the time you make contact with the ball, you've generated a lot of force along this chain. For this reason you need to develop strength in your lower extremities—your legs—so your push-off will be strong. From your serve to your low volleys to even the first step after a wide ball, your game relies on power in your legs. The following exercises will strengthen these:

- Back squat
- Bench step-up
- Calf raise (machine)
- Calf raise (seated)
- Leg curl (facedown)
- Leg press

On the same principle, developing hip and thigh muscles will improve your ability to change direction quickly. Lunges will help you reduce injuries to your groin. They'll also improve your side shuffling, playing in the ready position, and stability in grabbing those low volleys. These exercises will do this:

- Cross-over lunge
- Front lunge
- 45-Degree lunge
- Side lunge
- Walking lunge

III • ABDOMINAL MUSCLES

Everything you do in tennis revolves around your abdominal muscles. Strengthening your abdominals, trunk, and upper extremities will

(continued)

Table 1.1 *(continued)*

improve your range of motion and torque. The medicine ball exercises described in chapter 4 simulate ground strokes and overheads and train your muscles more specifically than any other strengthening workout:

- Bench step-up and press
- Drop pass
- Kneeling side throw
- Overhead throw
- Pullover toss

IV • TRUNK

You need a quick start on court, and these exercises will help develop one. They work to support the low back, helping in injury prevention. They also play an important role in maintaining range of motion and strength for serves and overheads. To condition the trunk chapter 3 offers you these exercises:

- Back extension
- Bicycle
- Glute-ham raise
- Hip press-up
- Hip roll
- Hip rotation
- Knee pull-in
- Russian twist
- Side sit-up
- Sit-up with legs raised

V • UPPER EXTREMITIES

You can't play tennis if you can't hold on to your racket. As your opponents increase the power of their shots, you need to strengthen your grip to fight back. Wrist exercises will not only build strength, they'll also condition the muscles of the forearm to absorb the impact from ball contact. This will decrease your chances of injuries from overuse, such as tennis elbow. The exercises are:

- Wrist flexion/extension
- Wrist pronation/supination
- Wrist ulnar/radial flexion

All the twisting and turning you do in the course of a day on court puts your body through a rigorous workout. Shoulder girdle exercises develop the muscles connecting the shoulder to the trunk. These exercises will help keep your ground strokes and overheads powerful while also preventing injuries resulting from your follow-through or extreme reach shots:

- Upright row
- Seated row
- Push press
- Pullover and press
- Pullover
- Front and back pulldown
- Pec dec
- Prone fly
- Dumbbell row
- Bench press
- Incline press (barbell)

(continued)

The muscles of the shoulder have very little to do with actually producing velocity in your strokes, but they're most important in stabilizing the shoulder during impact with the ball. Injury prevention is a key factor in shoulder exercises. If your arsenal is based on power tennis, you first have to prepare your body for battle by means of these exercises:

- Arm circles
- External/internal rotation (faceup)
- External shoulder rotation (seated)
- External shoulder rotation (on side)
- Front raise
- Side lateral raise

VI • TOTAL BODY

Some of your movements on court include a variety of elements. Exploding into a return of serve or moving from a split step into a volley requires several muscles or muscle groups to work together. These exercises, described in chapter 3, work both upper and lower extremities to develop the total body strength required for these skilled movement patterns:

- Dumbbell split jerk
- Front squat to push press

Number of Repetitions

How many repetitions (reps) of each exercise should you perform? The number of reps determines the degree of muscle tension. If you can perform only one rep with a specific weight for an exercise, the muscle tension is high. If you can perform two reps, the muscle tension is lower. Depending on the speed at which an exercise is performed, lower reps tend to create greater gains in power. Also, to avoid injury you should not perform isolation (single-joint) exercises for fewer reps, such as performing single-rep sets for biceps curls. I have planned the numbers of reps in these workouts very carefully.

Number of Sets

How many sets of each exercise should you perform? The number of sets should be inversely proportionate to the number of reps. If the reps are high (10 or more), then fewer sets are needed. So, if you are a beginner and 10 reps are prescribed for an exercise, you may only need to perform two sets to achieve an optimal training effect. If three reps are prescribed, four or more sets may be required. The number of sets is also determined by your training experience. To make continued progress, more experienced athletes require additional sets.

Tempo

At what speed should you perform each exercise? You will gain power more readily if you vary the tempo from exercise to exercise. The exception is speed development exercises (plyometrics). Plyometrics must always be performed at maximum speed, explosively.

Rest Intervals

How much rest time should you take between sets? When you train with heavy weights on multijoint exercises your nervous system needs more time to recover than when you train with lighter weight on single-joint exercises. For example, you may need to rest up to 5 minutes between sets of heavy power cleans but only 1 minute between sets of biceps curls. Another general rule about rest intervals is that larger muscle groups require longer rest intervals than smaller muscle groups. Also, when performing complexes (a technique in which you alternate between two exercises in the same workout) it is usually best to keep the rest interval as short as possible. I have applied these principles in planning the rest intervals in the Power Tennis Training program.

Resistance

How much resistance (weight) should you use for each exercise? This is determined by the number of repetitions prescribed for the particular exercise. Let's say you can perform one rep of an exercise with 100 pounds, but your workout plan calls for five repetitions. Instead of calculating percentages (see the appendix), just use a weight that you know will permit you to perform five reps. In other words, let the reps determine the resistance. At first this will be difficult, but training experience will enable you to determine how much weight you can handle after your first warm-up set.

Variety

When should you change your workout? Because the body is a very adaptive organism, workouts must be changed frequently to avoid staleness. This variety can be gained by changing the number of reps and sets, the exercises, and the tempo of the exercises. In Power Tennis Training these workout variables are constantly changing to provide maximum variety.

CHAPTER
2

WARM-UP AND STRETCHING EXERCISES

The **standard warm-up** for all Power Tennis Training workouts consists of the following three parts:

1. The **general warm-up** raises your body temperature and respiration. It consists of at least 5 minutes of an aerobic activity, like jogging or bicycling. It doesn't matter which aerobic exercise you choose so long as you break a sweat.
2. The **specific warm-up** prepares the muscles used in tennis that receive the most stress, especially the shoulder muscles. Because the shoulder is such a complex structure, you must perform several exercises for it. Heavy weights are not necessary; just be certain to get a full range of motion with each exercise.
3. The **shoulder and wrist/forearm stretches** will develop and maintain flexibility in those areas. For best results, perform these stretches after your shoulders have been thoroughly prepared with both a general and a specific warm-up.

Table 2.1 shows how I've organized the entire warm-up program:

Table 2.1	The Standard Warm-Up for Power Tennis Training Workouts

PART I • GENERAL WARM-UP

EXERCISE	DURATION/REPS
Jog, bike, stair-step, or rowing machine	5 min (easy)

PART II • SPECIFIC WARM-UP

EXERCISE	DURATION/REPS
Side lateral raise	10 reps
Front raise	10 reps
External/internal rotation (faceup)	10 reps
Prone fly	10 reps
Arm circles	20 reps (each direction)

PART III • SHOULDER AND WRIST/FOREARM STRETCHES

EXERCISE	DURATION/REPS
Shoulder stretch 1	15-30 sec
Shoulder stretch 2	15-30 sec
Wrist/forearm stretch	15-30 sec

● Warm-Up Exercises

Just a quick reminder:

Q: Why do we go through all of this conditioning?

A: *To improve performance and prevent injury. Before you begin the complex training workout, your muscles must be warmed up and properly stretched.*

To begin with, you should perform 5 to 10 minutes of aerobi (continuous) exercise before every workout to raise your body temperature and respiration to the intensity level required to perform your workout safely and efficiently. This type of warm-up, which I call the *general warm-up*, includes activities such as walking, rowing, and bicycling.

In addition to the general warm-up, the standard warm-up includes several specific warm-up exercises, which are demonstrated on the following pages. These exercises are designed to warm up areas of the body used extensively in tennis.

SIDE LATERAL RAISE

PURPOSE:

To warm up and strengthen the muscles on the side of the shoulders, which are used during the backhand.

PERFORMANCE:

Hold a dumbbell in each hand and rest them at your sides, palms facing each other. Keep your arms straight but not hyperextended. Lift the dumbbells to the sides until they are at least parallel to the floor, then slowly return them to the start. Do not lean forward or backward during the movement or try to use your legs to help you lift the weights. For the standard warm-up, perform a set of 10.

POINTERS:

Because this exercise effectively isolates the muscles on the side of the shoulders, heavy weights cannot be used. There is a tendency to make this exercise easier by allowing the arms to drift in front of the body. Avoid this, because it reduces the effectiveness of the exercise.

To perform this exercise on a cabled weight machine, stand to one side of a low pulley row and grasp the handle with the hand farther from the machine. The cable can be positioned either in front of or behind your chest. Lift the resistance to the side until your arms are at least parallel to the floor.

FRONT RAISE

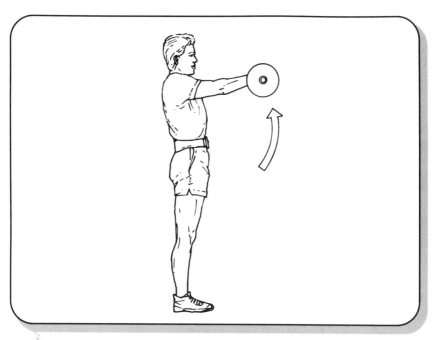

PURPOSE:

To warm up and strengthen the front shoulder muscles, which help produce power for the backhand.

PERFORMANCE:

Hold two dumbbells on your thighs, palms down, with your arms slightly bent. Lift the weights forward with your arms straight until they are parallel to the floor or slightly higher. Slowly return to the start. Do not arch backward during the exercise. You can also perform the movement by raising the weights alternately. For the standard warm-up, perform a set of 10.

POINTERS:

Avoid the tendency to turn the palms up during the movement as this will involve other muscle groups. Also, wearing a weight-lifting belt will help you maintain good posture.

EXTERNAL/INTERNAL ROTATION (FACEUP)

PURPOSE: To warm up and strengthen the internal and external rotator cuff muscles. These muscles help produce control while serving.

PERFORMANCE: Lie on your back and hold a dumbbell in your left hand. Place your upper arm perpendicular to your shoulders and bend your lower arm to a 45-degree angle. Placing a small towel under your elbow will make this exercise more comfortable. From this starting position, rotate your lower arm backward and forward as shown. For the standard warm-up, perform a set of 10.

POINTERS: Use light weights for this exercise and perform it slowly.

PRONE FLY

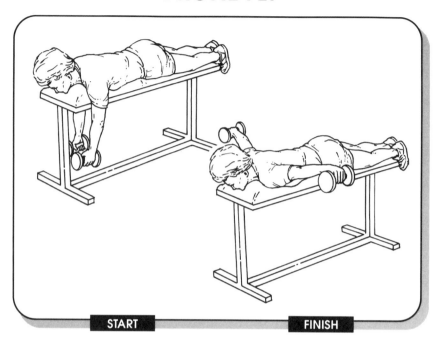

START   **FINISH**

PURPOSE:
To warm up and strengthen the upper back and rear shoulder muscles, which are used during the backhand.

PERFORMANCE:
Lie facedown on a narrow bench holding a dumbbell in each hand, or stand and bend forward from your waist. The palms should face each other at the start and the arms should be straight. Hold your breath and lift the weights to the finish position (slightly higher than horizontal). Exhale and slowly return to the start. For the standard warm-up, perform a set of 10.

POINTERS:
Do not hyperextend your elbows or arch upward at the finish of the exercise in an attempt to use more weight. Also, keep your arms in line with your shoulders during the exercise. Allowing your arms to drift forward may enable you to use more weight, but it changes the effect of the movement.

Because your back is supported during this exercise, it is recommended for those with a back injury.

ARM CIRCLES

PURPOSE: To warm up the shoulder and upper back muscles.

PERFORMANCE: Stand with your feet shoulder-width apart and your arms extended, parallel to floor. Make small circles forward and backward as shown. For the standard warm-up, perform a set of 20 (each direction).

POINTERS: This exercise can also be performed by holding light weight plates or dumbbells (about 2-1/2 pounds) in each hand. When holding weights during this exercise, be certain to keep the arms slightly bent to minimize the stress on your elbows.

● Stretching Movements

You should perform all preworkout stretches after the general and specific warm-up exercises. You should perform the postworkout stretches after every workout to prevent muscle tightness. Follow the instructions on the worksheet provided for these movements.

Preworkout Stretches

The following pages demonstrate the

- Shoulder Stretch 1
- Shoulder Stretch 2
- Wrist/Forearm Stretch

Postworkout Stretches

After illustrations of the three preworkout stretches you will find a series of postworkout stretches designed to stretch these body parts:

- Ankles
- Back
- Groin
- Hamstrings
- Hips
- Neck
- Quadriceps
- Shoulders
- Torso (abdominal muscles)
- Wrists and forearms

SHOULDER STRETCH 1

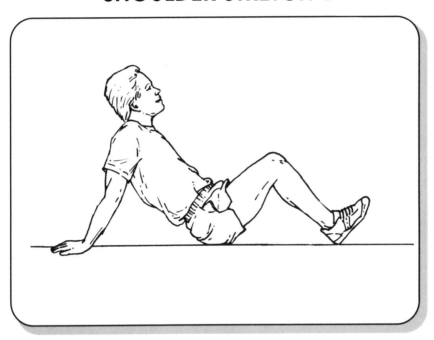

PURPOSE: To stretch the shoulder muscles.

PERFORMANCE: Lie faceup with your arms placed behind you as shown. Inch forward as far as comfortable and hold for 15 to 30 seconds.

POINTERS: Do not stretch to the point of pain!

SHOULDER STRETCH 2

PURPOSE: To stretch the shoulder muscles.

PERFORMANCE: Stand in front of a wall and assume the position shown. With your hands on the wall, lean forward from the waist as far as is comfortable and hold for 15 to 30 seconds.

POINTERS: Do not stretch to the point of pain!

WRIST/FOREARM STRETCH

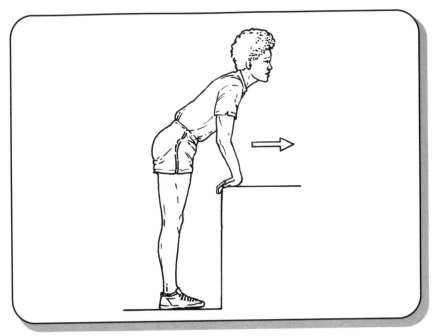

PURPOSE: To stretch the wrist and forearm muscles.

PERFORMANCE: Assume the position shown with your hands placed on a sturdy table or bench. Lean forward as far as is comfortable and hold for 15 to 30 seconds.

POINTERS: Do not stretch to the point of pain!

POSTWORKOUT STRETCHES

PURPOSE: To prevent muscle tightness after a workout.

PERFORMANCE: Assume the positions shown below. Move slowly into each posture until you feel a gentle stretch. Hold each position for at least 15 seconds before slowly releasing the stretch and moving on to the next one.

POINTERS: Breathe through your nose during each stretch. Don't rush through your cool-down.

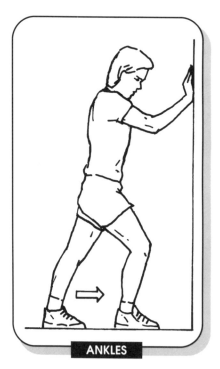

ANKLES

ANKLES

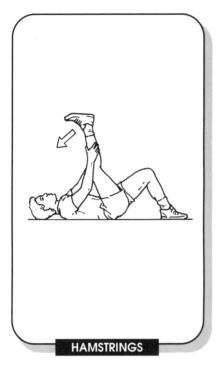

HAMSTRINGS

GROIN

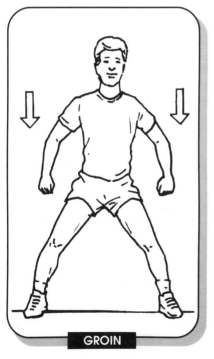

GROIN

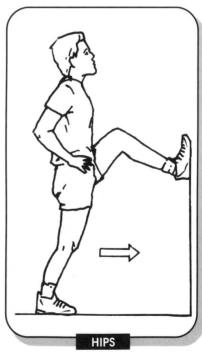

HIPS

HIPS

TORSO

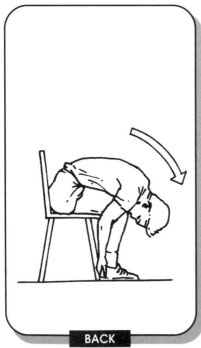

BACK

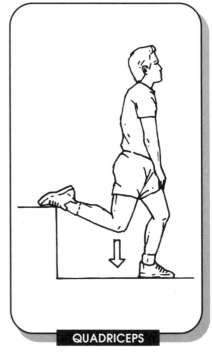

QUADRICEPS

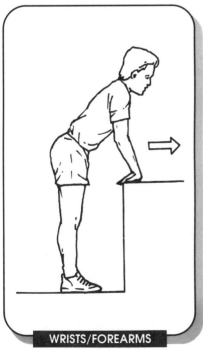

SHOULDERS

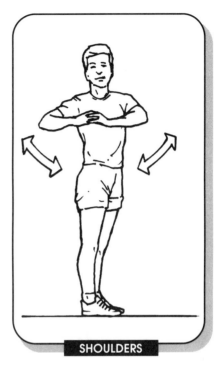

SHOULDERS

WRISTS/FOREARMS

NECK

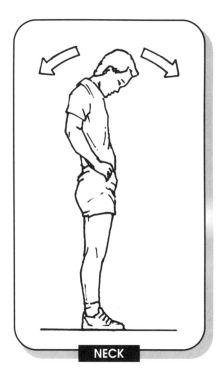

NECK

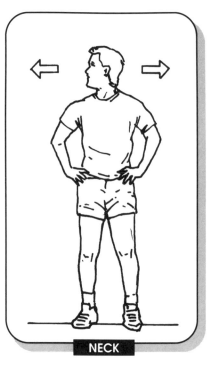

NECK

CHAPTER 3

WEIGHT TRAINING AND TRUNK EXERCISES

The first part of this chapter offers you general performance guidelines for using free weights and machines and then describes the weight training exercises best suited for tennis training. Then I move on to a discussion of eight trunk exercises that will help you add force to your ground strokes.

● General Performance Guidelines: Free Weights

Free weight equipment includes barbells, dumbbells, and accessory equipment like benches, squat racks, and curl benches. Free weight equipment offers a greater variety of exercises than weight machines and more effectively works the muscles that stabilize the joints.

All free weight equipment should be sturdy, contain no sharp corners, and have firm padding. A flat bench usually stands about 18 inches high and 12 inches wide. For the bench press exercise the bench should be high enough that you can place your feet flat on the floor without arching your back. It should be wide enough that the bench doesn't dig into your shoulders. Squat racks should be adjustable or set at a height 2 to 4 inches below shoulder level.

Wear a weight training belt when you use heavy weights or lift weights overhead. A weight training belt supports the trunk (torso) by helping to compress the gases and fluids in the abdominal cavity. This intra-abdominal pressure reduces compressive forces that stress the spine. A belt also encourages good technique by helping you maintain an upright posture.

⬤ General Performance Guidelines: Machines

Exercise machines won't make your workouts easier, but their appealing designs and convenient weight selection devices can make weight training more enjoyable. Machines also encourage proper form, and their ability to isolate specific muscles makes them valuable for injury rehabilitation.

The primary advantage that machines have over free weights is safety—the weights cannot drop or fall on you. If you're a beginner you'll find this feature especially reassuring since your muscles are just learning the techniques of the exercises. But, as with all exercises, proper instruction is necessary to decrease the likelihood of injuries and ensure maximum effectiveness. Don't let the natural safety advantages of machines lull you into a false sense of security.

If your gym has exercise machines you have never used, avoid experimentation. Insist that an instructor work one-on-one with you so you can derive maximum benefit from the exercises. Because every machine has its own peculiarities, ask the experts about these machines rather than try to figure them out for yourself. And if you have a chronic injury, you may need to avoid certain exercise machines that aggravate the condition. If seat belts are available on the machine, use them. Also, read all warning signs and additional instructions provided on a machine. Finally, do not use any machine that is not functioning smoothly, and report the problem to the appropriate personnel.

A few performance guidelines apply to almost every exercise machine. Your body must be properly fitted into a machine before you perform an exercise. You should always position yourself in a straight, aligned manner. On machines with adjustable seats and backrests, align the center of the body part you're working with the center of the pulley apparatus. Avoid twisting or shifting your weight during any exercise. If a machine has handgrips, do not squeeze them during the exercise; grasp them with a loose, comfortable grip. Also, avoid any sudden or jerky movements.

Avoid the tendency to rush through an exercise when using workouts to improve cardiovascular fitness, such as with circuit training. For most machine exercises it should take you twice as long to lower the weight (eccentric work) as it does to raise it (concentric work). For example, lift to the count of three . . . pause . . . and lower to the count of six. The reason I often prescribe this method of training for machines is that momentum can build up in the linkage of the machine. This may cause the resistance to move your limbs beyond their normal range of motion or at a speed you can't safely control. Bouncing a weight at the start or finish positions of an exercise can cause your lower back to round, creating an environment for injury.

Avoid the tendency to lean forward or to arch or round your lower back when using equipment that has you exercising in a seated position. Again, I recommend you wear a weight training belt as it encourages you to concentrate on maintaining good posture during an exercise. A belt will also reduce the potentially harmful compressive forces on the back during standing calf raises on a machine.

Use towels or extra seat pads when needed. A towel placed under your hips may help reduce the stress on the lower back during the prone (facedown) leg curl exercise. An extra seat pad or towel behind your lower back may prevent harmful arching of the lower back during the leg press exercise.

● Weight Training Exercises

The following pages illustrate the weight training exercises that will be a large part of your Power Tennis Training workouts described in Part II of this book. I have chosen only those exercises that are beneficial for tennis players' needs.

BACK EXTENSION

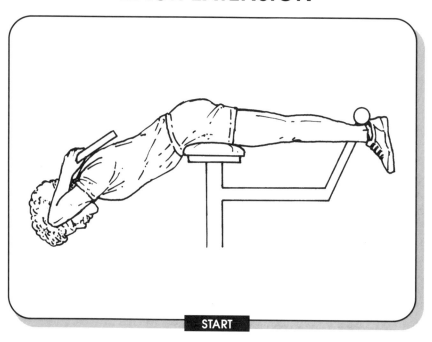

START

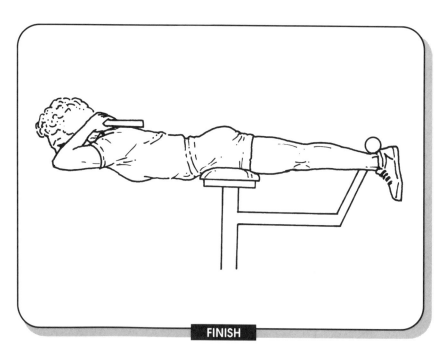

FINISH

PURPOSE: To strengthen the lower back, rear hip, and rear leg muscles.

PERFORMANCE: Assume the starting position shown on a back extension bench. Most benches have a pad above your ankles (to prevent you raising your legs) and a footpad (to prevent your slipping forward). If you do not have access to a back extension bench, lie facedown with your hips over the edge of a bench or sturdy table and have someone hold your legs while you perform the movement. Placing a rolled-up towel under your hips often makes this variation more comfortable.

Begin by bending as far forward as possible (without rounding your back), then arch back to the start position and up to the finish position. At the finish, your back should extend no higher than parallel to the floor.

POINTERS: Most athletes perform this exercise without using any resistance other than their own body weight. This is fine when you're just learning the exercise, but for maximum results you need to make it harder by holding weight plates or barbells on your shoulders or across your chest.

BACK SQUAT

START/FINISH

MID-POINT

PURPOSE: To strengthen all the major muscles of the lower body (the source of most of the power in tennis).

PERFORMANCE: With a barbell resting behind your neck, spread your feet shoulder-width apart and point your toes slightly out (start). Take a deep breath and bend your legs in a slow, controlled manner until the tops of your thighs are at least parallel to the floor (mid-point). During the descent keep your back flat, chest out, and your eyes focused slightly downward or directly ahead. Drive back to the start, exhaling when your legs are nearly straight. During the ascent look directly ahead or slightly up.

POINTERS: Some instructors believe the back squat can harm the knees. Such belief is unfounded. Any problem that arises from the squat is usually from lower back strain. Strong abdominal muscles help prevent this.

By varying your foot position, you can change the effect of this exercise on the muscles. A narrow stance (feet about 8 inches apart) emphasizes the front of the thighs and a wider stance emphasizes the hips, buttocks, and inner thighs.

BENCH PRESS

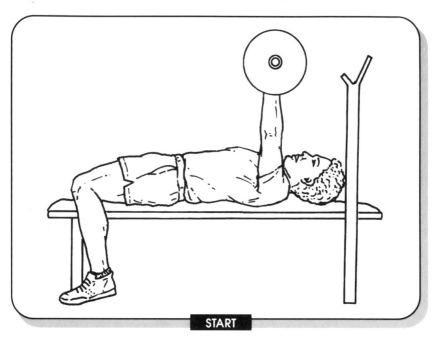

START

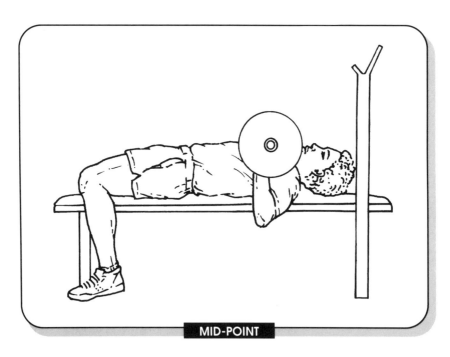

MID-POINT

PURPOSE:

To strengthen the chest, triceps, and front shoulder muscles.

PERFORMANCE:

Lie faceup on a bench press bench with your feet flat on the floor, straddling the bench with your feet shoulder-width apart. Remove the barbell from the supports so it is suspended directly above your throat. Your wrists should be positioned over your elbows (start). Take a deep breath and lower the weight to your mid-chest, or slightly lower if you're a female (mid-point). Without bouncing the weight off your chest, press it back to the start, exhaling when your arms are nearly straight.

POINTERS:

The bench press can be performed with barbells and dumbbells and with various grips. A wider grip emphasizes the chest, and a closer grip emphasizes the shoulders and triceps. (Note: With a wide grip your elbows will face away from your body, and with a narrow grip your elbows will tend to be drawn into your sides.)

With dumbbells you can perform this exercise through a greater range of motion. For this variation you should hold the dumbbells so the inside plates are facing each other (palms facing your knees). When pressing the weights overhead, bring them together until the inside plates touch at the finish. Also, always have spotters available when using heavy weights on this exercise. And although it may help you lift more weight (by placing your chest in a stronger leverage position), do not arch your back at any time during the lift.

BENCH STEP-UP

START

FINISH

PURPOSE: To strengthen the front and rear thigh muscles with minimal stress on the lower back.

PERFORMANCE: Remove a barbell from supports, holding it behind your head. Place one foot on the box, keeping the rear foot as close as possible to the box (start). Straighten your front leg, allowing the rear foot to drag along the edge of the box, until you reach the finish position shown with the front leg straight *but not locked.* Slowly lower to the start. It is not necessary to step onto the box with the rear leg. Also, always keep the rear knee slightly bent during the exercise to improve balance.

This exercise can also be performed by holding the barbell in front of the chest or by holding dumbbells at your sides. Because a substantial amount of weight can be used in this exercise, weight-lifting straps may be used to hold the bar in place.

POINTERS: A high box emphasizes the rear hip and rear leg muscles, and a low box emphasizes the front leg muscles. A high box is set so your upper thigh is parallel to the floor; a low box should be roughly half that size (10 inches is about average).

The safest way to perform this exercise is from inside a power rack. If such a rack is not available, you should have at least one spotter standing behind you. If a spotter or power rack is not available, it would be better to perform this exercise with dumbbells or substitute another leg exercise for it.

CALF RAISE (MACHINE)

PURPOSE:

To strengthen the calf muscles (gastrocnemius and soleus). Staying on the balls of your feet while playing tennis can be especially tiring for the calf muscles; this exercise will help build your resistance to fatigue.

PERFORMANCE:

Place your feet on the edge of the machine so that your heels extend lower than the balls of your feet. Place your shoulders under the pads by flexing your legs—the pads should be positioned lower than your shoulders. Keeping your back flat, straighten your legs to assume the start position shown. Perform the exercise by lowering and raising your heels through as great a range of motion as possible. Do not bend forward at any time.

POINTERS:

Perform this exercise in a slow, controlled manner—avoid bouncing. It might also help to wear a weight-lifting belt.

Varying your toe position (in or out) will emphasize different areas of the calf, as will using wider or narrower stances. Bending your knees slightly while performing the exercise will provide additional variety.

CALF RAISE (SEATED)

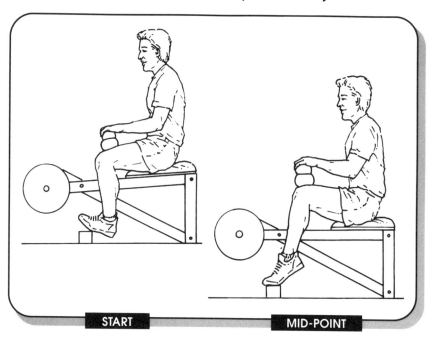

START   MID-POINT

PURPOSE: To strengthen the lower portion of the calf (soleus).

PERFORMANCE: Assume the starting position shown so that your heels can extend lower than the balls of your feet. Keep your toes pointed straight ahead; let your heels drop as far down as possible, stretching the calves to their full length (start). Begin the exercise by rising on your toes as high as possible (mid-point), pause, then return to the start.

POINTERS: Perform this exercise in a slow, controlled manner. Avoid bouncing.

Varying your toe position (in or out) will emphasize different areas of the calf, as will using a wider or narrower stance. You can also perform cheating repetitions by using your arms to assist you with weights that would otherwise be too heavy for you. Some seated calf machines have convenient handles on the knee pad for this purpose.

CROSS-OVER LUNGE

PURPOSE: To strengthen and improve flexibility in the inner and outer thigh muscles.

PERFORMANCE: From a standing position, place a barbell behind your neck. With your right foot, step to your left so that your right leg crosses in front of your left. From this position bend your knees as far as comfortable. Return to the start. Perform the required number of repetitions with your right leg before switching legs.

POINTERS: Your flexibility will improve as you perform this exercise, so don't be concerned if you have a limited range of motion at first.

For safety, it's important to wear sturdy footwear such as a cross-training or weight-lifting shoe.

DUMBBELL ROW

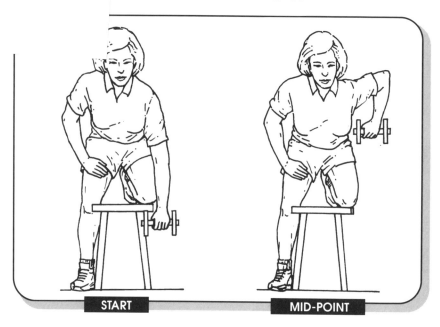

| START | MID-POINT |

PURPOSE:

To strengthen the triceps and the muscles of the center of the back, used to help generate power during a backhand.

PERFORMANCE:

With one arm braced in front of you and one knee resting on a bench, grasp a dumbbell with your free hand and let it hang over one edge (start). Hold your breath and begin the movement by pulling the dumbbell to your upper chest so that your elbow is higher than your chest (mid-point). Pause briefly in this position, then exhale as you slowly lower the weight back to the start.

Avoid the tendency to jerk the weight upward by arching your back. Also, do not allow your palms to turn inward during the exercise.

POINTERS:

When using a heavy weight, you may need to support your grip with straps. Weight gloves also improve your grip. Because your lower back is supported and a relatively light weight is used, this exercise is unlikely to cause or aggravate lower back problems.

DUMBBELL SPLIT JERK

PURPOSE: To develop total body power and coordination.

PERFORMANCE: Hold a dumbbell in each hand and lift them to your shoulders, palms facing away from your body. Flex your knees slightly and then thrust the weights overhead while splitting your legs as shown. Return to the start and repeat using the opposite leg as the forward leg to complete one repetition.

POINTERS: Because this exercise requires considerable practice to perfect, when you first perform it use very light weights.

TERNAL SHOULDER ROTATION
(ON SIDE)

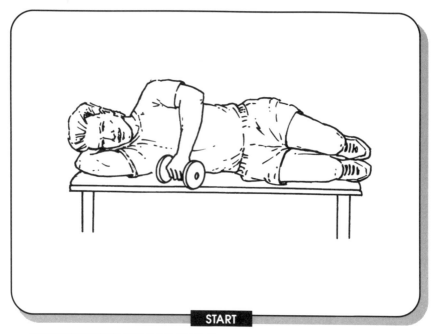

START

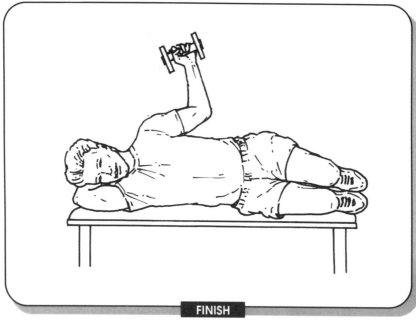

FINISH

PURPOSE: To strengthen the muscles that externally rotate the shoulders. These muscles provide control in serving and power for the backhand.

PERFORMANCE: Assume the starting position shown, with a dumbbell in your left hand. Lift the weight to the finish position shown. Repeat using your right hand.

POINTERS: Use light weights for this exercise and perform it slowly.

ʹERNAL SHOULDER ROTATION (SEATED)

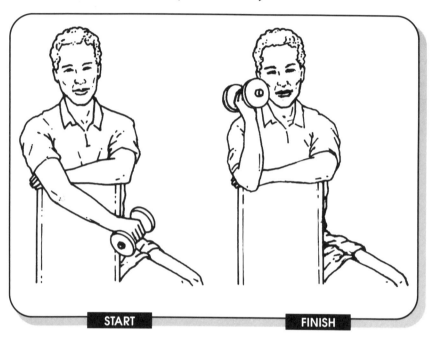

START   **FINISH**

PURPOSE: To strengthen the muscles that externally rotate the shoulders. These muscles provide control in serving and power for the backhand.

PERFORMANCE: Assume the starting position shown, with a dumbbell in your right hand. Lift the weight to the finish position shown. Repeat using your left hand.

POINTERS: Use light weights on this exercise and perform it slowly.

45-DEGREE LUNGE

PURPOSE: To strengthen the inner and outer thigh muscles and to improve flexibility in these areas.

PERFORMANCE: From a standing position, place a barbell behind your back. Step 45 degrees to your left and then sink into the squat position shown. The left foot should be slightly pointed out, in line with the knee, as much as possible. Push off with your left leg and then step back to the start. Perform the same movement to the other direction.

POINTERS: Your flexibility will improve as you perform this exercise, so don't be concerned if you have a limited range of motion at first.

For safety, it's important to wear sturdy footwear such as a cross-trainer or weight-lifting shoe. Do not allow the knee to move in front of the toes, as this will place harmful stress on the knee.

FRONT AND BACK PULLDOWN

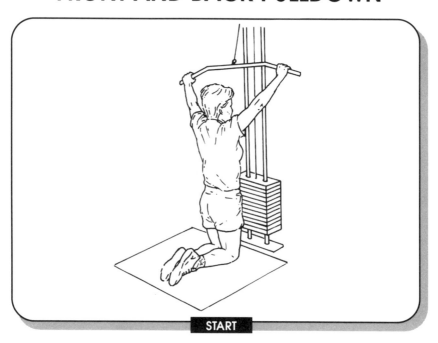

START

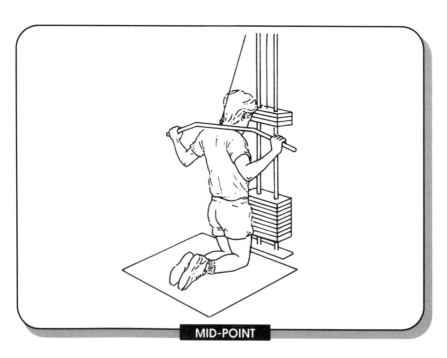

MID-POINT

PURPOSE:

To strengthen the upper back muscles known as the latissimus dorsi (lats) and, to a lesser extent, the biceps. These muscles help provide stability during stroking.

PERFORMANCE:

Grasp the bar with a wide grip, palms facing away from you. Your arms should be straight but not locked (start). Pull the bar to the base of your neck by first retracting your shoulders and then following through with your arms (mid-point). Pause momentarily in this position before slowly returning the bar to the start. When performing this exercise in front, pull the bar to your collarbone while leaning back slightly, arching your chest.

POINTERS:

When this exercise is performed behind the neck, the upper back muscles known as the trapezius receive more work. A closer grip places more emphasis on the biceps as does a grip with the palms facing you. A closer grip also emphasizes the lower lat muscles.

Many gyms offer several bar attachments for each pulldown variation. The handle shown is the most comfortable for wide grip pulldowns.

FRONT LUNGE

PURPOSE:

To strengthen the lower leg muscles (quadriceps and hamstrings) and improve hip flexibility. This exercise will also improve quickness and control for lunging movements.

PERFORMANCE:

Hold a barbell on your chest (remove it from supports) and place your feet about 6 inches apart. From this starting position, take a big step forward and lower your body to the position shown. Return to the start by shifting your weight backward, straightening your front leg, and taking several small steps back to the start. Perform the next lunge with your other leg as the front leg. Keep your back vertical throughout the exercise.

POINTERS:

If you find it difficult to hold the barbell in this position, cross your hands in front, forming an "X."

Keep your rear leg relaxed throughout the exercise, and work toward eventually being able to touch your rear leg to the floor.

FRONT SQUAT TO PUSH PRESS

PURPOSE: To exercise the whole body and develop power.

PERFORMANCE: Place a barbell on your shoulders as shown in the first drawing. Bend your legs to the squat position shown in the second drawing. Without pausing, vigorously straighten your legs and thrust the weight overhead as shown in the last drawing.

POINTERS: Using a weight-lifting belt may help support your back and help you maintain good posture.

A

B

C

D

GLUTE-HAM RAISE

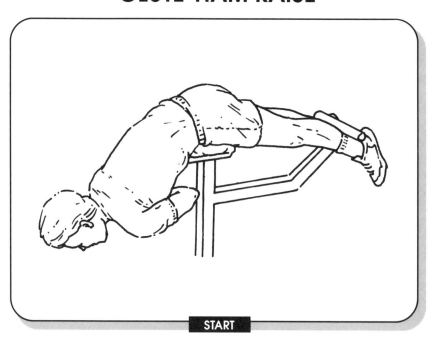

START

FINISH

PURPOSE: To strengthen the muscles of the lower back, rear hip (glutes), and back leg (hamstrings).

PERFORMANCE: On a back extension bench, assume the starting position shown. Most of these benches have a pad above your ankles (prevents you raising your legs) and a rear footpad (prevents you slipping forward). If you do not have access to a back extension bench, lie lengthwise on a bench or sturdy table and have someone hold your legs while you perform the movement. Placing a rolled-up towel under your hips often makes this variation more comfortable.

Perform the exercise by bending as far forward from the waist as possible (without rounding your back) and then arch back upward. When you reach parallel, continue the movement by bending your knees and lifting your torso to the position shown (finish). Reverse this procedure and bend forward to return to the start.

POINTERS: Most people who perform this exercise do so without using any resistance other than their own body weight. This is fine when you're just learning the exercise, but for maximum results you need to make it harder by holding weight plates or barbells on your shoulders or across your chest.

INCLINE PRESS (BARBELL)

START

MID-POINT

PURPOSE: To strengthen the upper chest muscles, triceps, and front shoulder muscles.

PERFORMANCE: Lie faceup on an incline bench with your feet flat on the floor. (If no seat is available, bend your knees slightly as shown.) Remove the barbell from the supports so it is suspended directly above your forehead (start). Lower the weight to a point just below your collarbone (mid-point) and then press it back to the start. Exhale when your arms are nearly straight.

POINTERS: The angle of the bench places more emphasis on the upper portion of the chest (compared to a horizontal bench press). A wider grip places more emphasis on the chest; a narrower grip places more emphasis on the shoulders and triceps. With a wide grip your elbows will face away from your body; with a narrower grip your elbows will tend to be drawn into your sides.

It's important to keep your lower body stable during this exercise by tensing the legs and hips. It may also help to try pushing your heels to the floor while pressing upward with your arms.

LEG CURL (FACEDOWN)

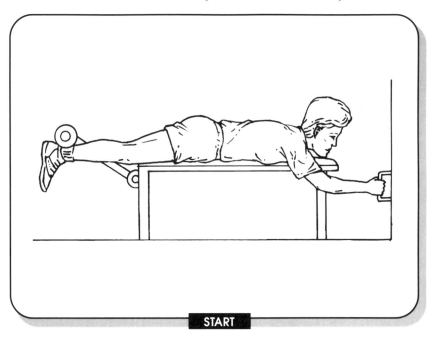

START

MID-POINT

PURPOSE:

To strengthen the rear leg muscles (hamstrings), especially the lower portion.

PERFORMANCE:

Assume the position shown in the first illustration. Your kneecaps should extend horizontally just over the edge of the bench, and the back of your ankles should rest against the padded bar. Do not hyperextend your knees!

Begin the exercise by bending your knees as far as possible, trying to touch the pad to your buttocks (mid-point); pause, then slowly return to the starting position. For maximum effectiveness, keep your hips flat against the bench throughout the movement. Raising the hips in an effort to use more weight restricts your range of motion and may place potentially harmful stress on the lower back.

POINTERS:

You can also perform this exercise on the type of bench that forms a slight "V" in the center. Placing a rolled-up towel under your hips may help reduce pressure on the lower back.

LEG PRESS

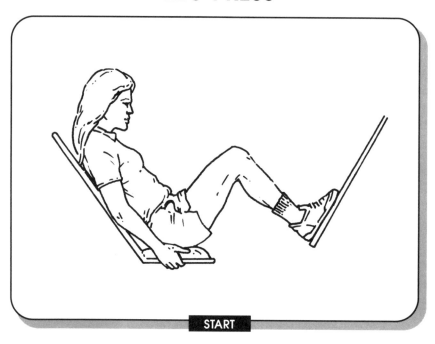

START

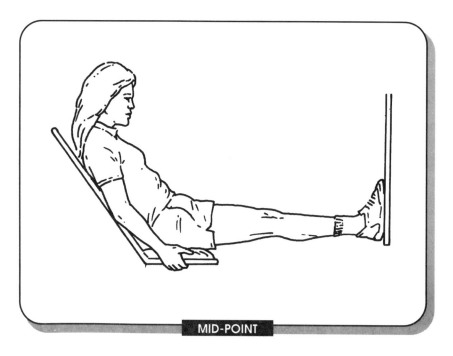

MID-POINT

PURPOSE: To strengthen all the major lower body muscles, especially the front leg muscles (quadriceps). Most of the power of your ground strokes comes from these muscles.

PERFORMANCE: Sit in the machine with your legs resting on the footpad as shown in the first illustration. Adjust the seat so that your lower and upper legs form a 90-degree angle. Your feet should be parallel to each other and about 6 inches apart. Take a deep breath and then press the weight forward, coming just short of locking your knees (mid-point). Lower the weight slowly and exhale as you return to start.

POINTERS: There are several types of leg press machines. Although they perform the same function, you can usually handle more weight on the angled versions.

Because the lower back is supported during this exercise, the leg press is a good exercise for those with back problems. However, be certain not to let your knees bend further than 90 degrees as this would cause your back to round, placing potentially harmful stress on the lower back.

This exercise can also be performed with one leg at a time.

PEC DEC

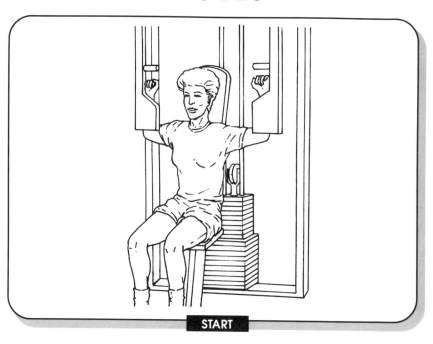

START

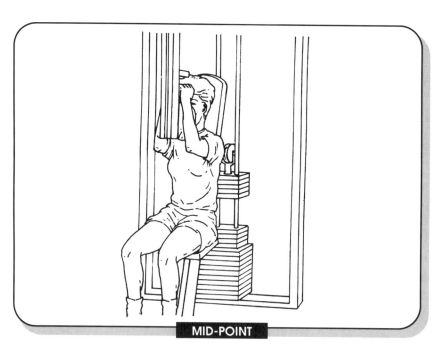

MID-POINT

PURPOSE:

To strengthen the center pectoral muscles without involving the triceps (as bench presses do). These muscles are used during the forehand.

PERFORMANCE:

Assume the starting position shown with your arms about parallel to the floor and your back flat against the backrest. Pull the pads together as far as possible, pause, and then slowly return to the start. It's important not to let your elbows extend beyond a point where they are in line with your shoulders. Such an extreme range of motion may cause stretch marks on the front of your shoulders or injure the joint.

POINTERS:

If you are training with a partner, it would be better to have him or her assist you by bringing the pads together before you begin. This lets you ease gradually into a comfortable stretched position for the first repetition. The tendency to jerk the pads together in the first repetition can injure the shoulders.

Some machines are equipped with a seat belt. Its function is to encourage good posture rather than to keep you from falling off the machine.

PULLOVER

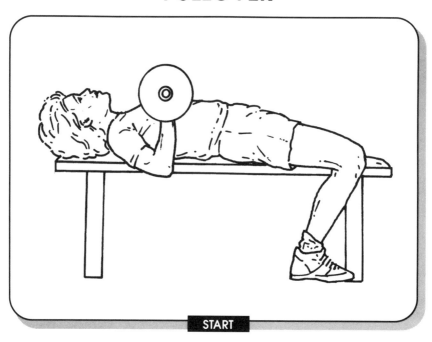

START

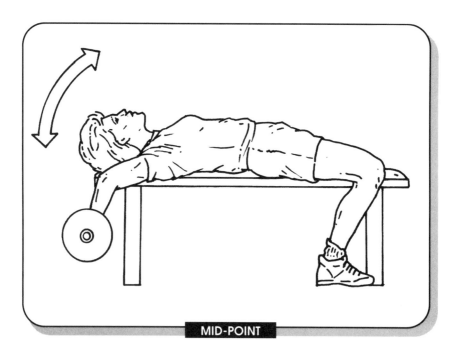

MID-POINT

PURPOSE:

To strengthen the upper back muscles as they function in serving.

PERFORMANCE:

Lie faceup on a narrow bench. Your head should be fully supported by the bench—do not let it hang over the edge.

To perform this exercise with a barbell, hold the weight with a shoulder-width grip, palms facing away from your body (start).

Keeping the weight as close to your head as possible, lower the weight to the mid-point shown and then pull it to the start. Inhale as you lower the weight, hold your breath as you raise it, and then exhale at the finish.

To perform this exercise with a dumbbell, hold a dumbbell with one end facing the ceiling. Rest the dumbbell on your chest. Your palms should be placed on the inside edge of the top plate and your thumbs should be wrapped around the sleeve. Lower the dumbbell in the manner described above and pull it back to the chest.

POINTERS:

Do not arch your back during this exercise.

ULLOVER AND PRESS

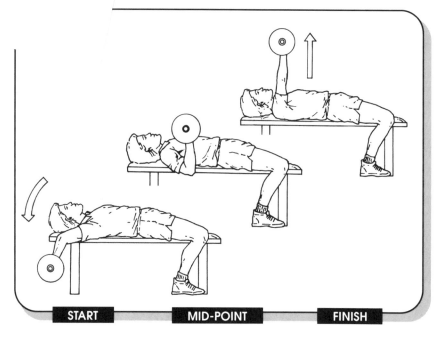

| START | MID-POINT | FINISH |

PURPOSE: To strengthen the upper back muscles and triceps as they function in serving.

PERFORMANCE: Lie faceup on a narrow bench and hold a barbell with a shoulder-width grip, palms facing away from your body as you would for a pullover. Your head should be fully supported by the bench—do not let it hang over the edge. Keeping the weight as close to your head as possible, pull the weight over the head to the mid-point position. From here press the weight to extended arms (finish) and then return to the start. Inhale as you lower the weight, hold your breath as you raise it, and then exhale at the mid-point position. At this point inhale and hold your breath as you press the weight overhead, and then exhale as you lower the weight.

POINTERS: Do not arch your back during this exercise.

PUSH PRESS

START　　　　　　**FINISH**

PURPOSE: To develop total body power and strengthen the shoulders and triceps. This exercise will improve jumping ability.

PERFORMANCE: Remove a barbell from a set of support racks, placing it on the shoulders as shown. Your elbows should be pointed slightly down and out. Keeping your chest high and abdominal muscles pulled in, bend your legs slightly (start) and thrust the weight overhead to straight arms (finish). Lower carefully to the start position.

POINTERS: This exercise can also be performed with the barbell behind your neck (as in the starting position for the back squat). This variation is recommended for those with extremely tight shoulders and wrists who find holding the bar in front uncomfortable.

SEATED ROW

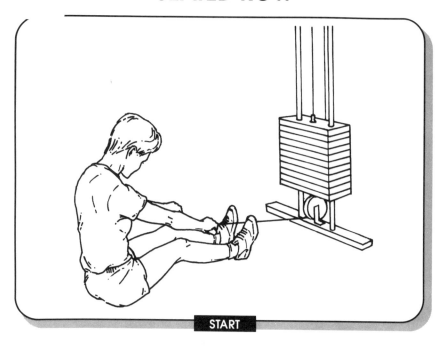

START

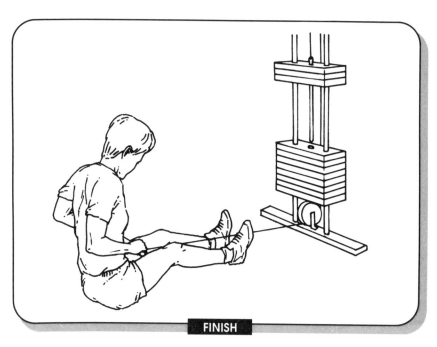

FINISH

PURPOSE:

To strengthen the center upper back muscles that are used during the backhand.

PERFORMANCE:

Sit in front of a row pulley machine with your knees slightly bent. Grasp the pulley bar with both hands, thumbs down (start). Begin by pulling your shoulders back, then follow through with your arms (finish). Slowly return to the start. Keep your elbows out to the sides (away from your body) when pulling.

POINTERS:

Avoid the tendency to lean backwards during the initial part of this exercise.

Many low pulley machines have rowing attachments for different grips. An attachment that has you grip with your palms facing each other (a neutral grip) may be more effective for developing the back muscles.

Some gyms have seated row machines that have chest pads to reduce the stress on the back. When using these machines, keep your chest in contact with the chest pad during the entire exercise.

SIDE LUNGE

PURPOSE:

To strengthen the inner and outer thigh muscles and to improve flexibility in these areas. This exercise helps develop lateral quickness and control during lunging movements.

PERFORMANCE:

From a standing position, place a barbell behind your neck. Step to your right and then sink into the squat position shown. The right foot should be slightly pointed out and in line with the knee. Push off with your right leg and then step back to the start. Perform the same movement in the other direction with the left leg.

POINTERS:

Your flexibility will improve as you perform this exercise, so don't be concerned if you have a limited range of motion when you first perform it.

For safety, it's important to wear sturdy footwear such as a cross-trainer or weight-lifting shoe. Do not point the foot you are stepping with forward as this will place harmful stress on the knee.

UPRIGHT ROW

START

FINISH

PURPOSE: To strengthen the upper back muscles known as the trapezius, a muscle group that provides stability during serving. This exercise will also help improve your grip.

PERFORMANCE: Grasp a barbell holding your palms down (start) and hands positioned 6 to 8 inches apart. Pull the weight up to your throat (finish) and then return to the start. During the exercise keep the barbell as close to your body as possible and your elbows up and out. You can also use dumbbells. If you do, hold the weight with your palms facing you and try to keep the inside edges of the plates touching throughout the movement. Also, avoid the tendency to cheat on this exercise by using the back or leg muscles.

POINTERS: Wrist straps will enable you to use heavier weights (without cheating) and a weight-lifting belt will encourage correct posture.

A narrow grip increases the range of motion of the upper back muscles. A wider grip will enable you to use more weight but reduces the effectiveness of the exercise.

WALKING LUNGE

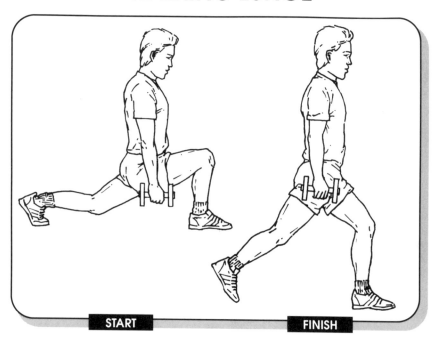

START **FINISH**

PURPOSE:

To strengthen and improve the flexibility of the hip and lower leg muscles. This exercise will help develop forward quickness.

PERFORMANCE:

Place a dumbbell in each hand and assume the split position shown (start). Your arms should be straight or slightly bent. Keeping your hips low, swing your left leg through to the finish position shown. Continue walking in this manner for the required distance or time, or the required number of repetitions or steps.

POINTERS:

As you become stronger in this exercise, you can place a barbell behind your head for resistance instead of holding dumbbells.

As you become tired in this exercise, there is a tendency to lift your hips or bounce up and down while stepping, actions that reduce the effectiveness of the exercise.

WRIST FLEXION/EXTENSION

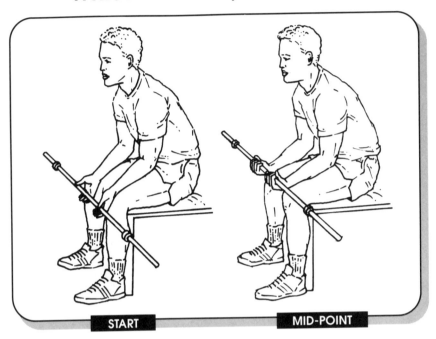

START   MID-POINT

PURPOSE: To strengthen the wrist and forearm muscles.

PERFORMANCE: Sit on the edge of a bench. Hold a barbell palms up, with your forearms resting on your knees. Let your wrist bend to the start position shown. Curl the weight upward (to the mid-point), pause, then slowly return the weight to the start. For the wrist extension exercise (not shown), hold the barbell palms down and curl the weight backward.

POINTERS: Do not let the weight roll down your fingertips during the wrist flexion exercise.

Although only a few gyms have them, a swingbell is an excellent piece of equipment for doing this exercise. A swingbell has the weight centered in the middle of the bar, making it easier to balance the weight during wrist curls.

WRIST PRONATION/SUPINATION

START   **FINISH**

PURPOSE: To strengthen the muscles of the wrist and forearms.

PERFORMANCE: Place a leverage bar in one hand and rest your forearms across a bench as shown. Slowly rotate the weight in the manner shown.

POINTERS: Very little weight is necessary to attain a training effect in this exercise, and even less weight is needed when a longer leverage bar is used.

Although it's possible to perform only wrist pronation or supination by limiting the range of motion of this exercise, it's more convenient to perform both exercises alternately by rotating the bar to your left and back to your right.

WRIST ULNAR/RADIAL FLEXION

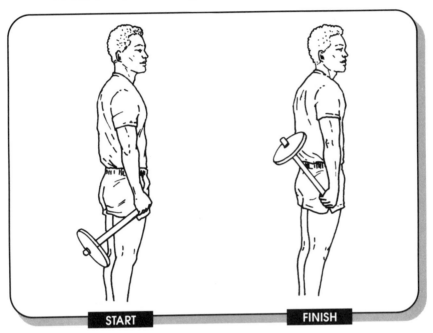

START **FINISH**

PURPOSE: To improve your grip by strengthening the wrist and forearm muscles.

PERFORMANCE: To perform ulnar flexion, place one end of a leverage bar in the position shown. Without moving the arm, turn your wrist backwards as far as possible (finish). Lower slowly and repeat.

To perform radial flexion (not shown), hold the bar so that the weight is pointing forward and up. From this starting position, turn your wrist forward as high as possible. Lower slowly and repeat.

POINTERS: Very little weight is necessary to get a training effect from this exercise. Also, a longer leverage bar requires even less weight because the resistance is further from the hand.

● Trunk Exercises

Your trunk muscles are involved in everything you do in tennis. Strengthening them will improve your range of motion and the torque forces (i.e., rotation forces) you create. This translates into faster and more powerful ground strokes. There is no doubt you will see a carryover to your overheads and volleys as well. In addition to the eight exercises shown on the following pages, the medicine ball exercises described in chapter 4 strengthen your trunk muscles.

BICYCLE

PURPOSE: To strengthen the trunk by using the quadriceps and hamstrings.

PERFORMANCE: Lie on your back and place your hands by your side (or underneath your tailbone). Flatten your back against the floor and maintain this position throughout the exercise. Extend your right leg and pull your left leg toward your chest. From this starting position make small circles with your feet as if riding a bicycle.

POINTERS: Do not hold your breath during this exercise. Concentrate on achieving a full range of motion with your legs.

HIP PRESS-UP

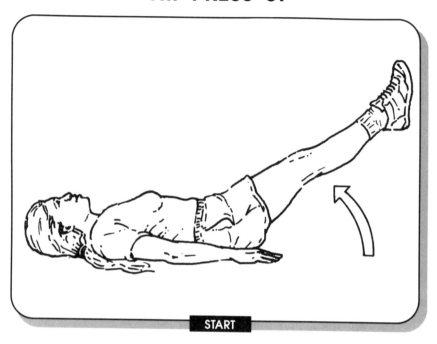

START

FINISH

PURPOSE: To strengthen the trunk by developing the lower abdominal muscles.

PERFORMANCE: Lie faceup on the floor with your hands at your sides (or under your tailbone). To assume the starting position, place your feet together and lift them until they are at a 45-degree angle as shown (start). Press your lower back to the floor and try to maintain this position with your back throughout the entire exercise. Begin by lifting your legs perpendicular to the floor and then raise your hips as high as possible (finish). Pause momentarily at the top before slowly returning to the start.

POINTERS: To increase the difficulty of this exercise, perform it at a slower pace, place your hands behind your head, or lie faceup on an incline sit-up board.

HIP ROLL

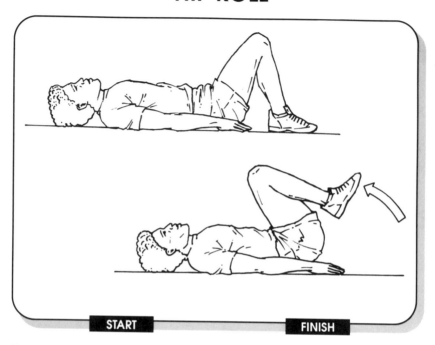

START **FINISH**

PURPOSE:
To strengthen the trunk by developing the lower abdominal muscles.

PERFORMANCE:
Lie faceup on the floor with your hands at your sides (or under your tailbone). Press your lower back to the floor and try to maintain this position with your back throughout the exercise (start). Keeping your knees bent, lift your legs to the finish position shown, pause, then slowly return to the start.

POINTERS:
To increase the difficulty of this exercise, perform it at a slower pace, place your hands behind your head, or lie faceup on an incline sit-up board.

HIP ROTATION

PURPOSE: To strengthen the trunk by developing the abdominal muscles on the sides of the waist (internal and external obliques).

PERFORMANCE: Lie faceup with your arms extended over your head. Keeping your feet together, lift your legs until they are perpendicular to the floor. Begin the exercise by lowering your legs to the right as far as is comfortable and then to the left. Do not lift your shoulders off the ground.

POINTERS: If this exercise is too difficult or creates discomfort at the back of your thighs, bend your knees slightly.

KNEE PULL-IN

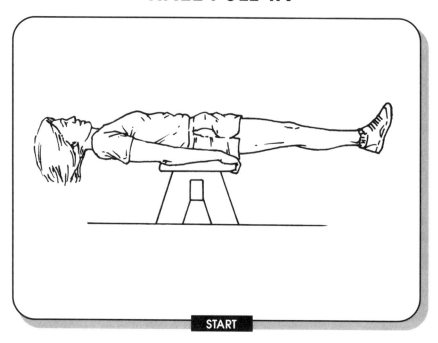

START

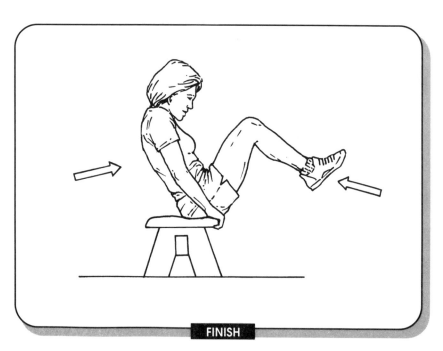

FINISH

PURPOSE: To strengthen the trunk by developing the abdominal muscles.

PERFORMANCE: Lie faceup across a sturdy bench as shown in the starting position. Pull your knees to your chest and your chest to your knees (finish). Reverse the procedure to return to the start.

POINTERS: Do not allow your head to drop below horizontal at any time during the exercise.

RUSSIAN TWIST

START

MID-POINT

PURPOSE: To strengthen the side abdominal muscles, prevent muscle imbalances in the trunk area, and develop powerful twisting movements.

PERFORMANCE: Lie faceup on a back extension bench. Most of these benches have a pad that rests above your ankles (preventing your legs from rising) and a rear footpad (preventing you from slipping forward). If you do not have access to a back extension bench, lie lengthwise on a bench and have someone hold your legs while you perform the movement.

Perform the exercise by leaning back to a 45-degree angle with your arms extended in the start position shown. Place your hands together or hold a small weight for added resistance. Twist 90 degrees to your left (mid-point). Then twist to the start and twist to your right and finally back to the start to complete one repetition.

POINTERS: At first perform this movement slowly (or throughout a smaller range of motion) until you are comfortable with the technique. Later, work on accelerating at the beginning portion of the exercise.

It's important to keep your body at a 45-degree angle during the movement. Stop performing the exercise if your technique breaks.

SIDE SIT-UP

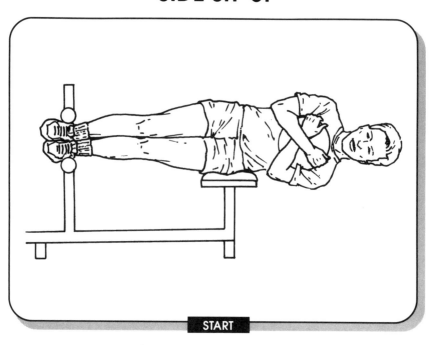

START

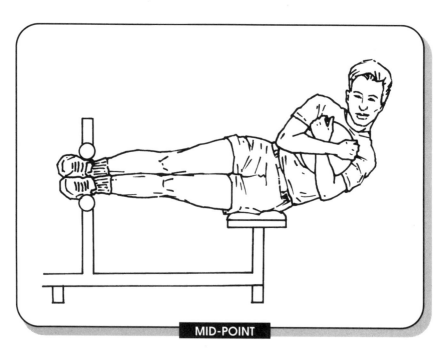

MID-POINT

PURPOSE: To strengthen the trunk by developing the side abdominal muscles.

PERFORMANCE: Assume the starting position shown on a back extension bench. Most of these benches have a pad that rests above your ankles (preventing your legs from rising) and a rear footpad (preventing you from slipping forward). If you do not have access to a back extension bench, lie lengthwise on a bench and have someone hold your legs while you perform the movement.

Perform the exercise by bending as far forward as possible and then lift your trunk to the mid-point position shown. Then, return to the start position. Do not arch your back when performing this exercise.

POINTERS: Most people who perform this exercise do so without using any weight other than their own body weight. This is fine when you're just learning the exercise, but to get maximum benefit you need to make it harder by holding weight plates across your chest.

You can also perform this exercise on the floor by having a partner hold your legs as you perform the movement.

SIT-UP WITH LEGS RAISED

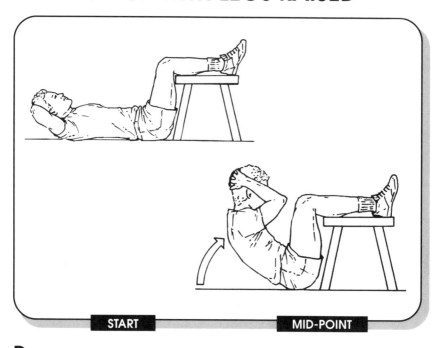

START   MID-POINT

PURPOSE: To strengthen the trunk by developing the abdominal muscles.

PERFORMANCE: Lie faceup and place your feet on a bench so that your thighs are perpendicular to the floor. Rest your hands on the side of your head (just behind your head with fingers locked). Flatten your back (start). Begin the exercise by lifting your shoulders to the mid-point position shown. Slowly return to the floor.

POINTERS: To minimize the involvement of the hip flexors (upper thigh muscles), this exercise must be performed slowly.

CHAPTER
4

PLYOMETRIC AND MEDICINE BALL EXERCISES

Plyometrics is special exercises that teach your muscles to produce maximum force faster. This chapter describes a dozen plyometric exercises used in the Power Tennis Training program. The five medicine ball exercises used in the program are also described. Utilizing a medicine ball helps to develop the trunk and upper extremities while using the legs to stabilize or start the activity. These exercises are very "tennis-specific" and allow exercisers to mimic many of the movements they will use on the court.

● Plyometric Exercises

Because plyometrics trains the nervous system, you must perform these exercises with maximum explosiveness. Always wear shoes with good support (such as a cross-trainer), exercise on soft landing surfaces (such as grass), and be certain that any boxes you use provide sufficient stability.

DEPTH JUMP
WITH LATERAL MOVEMENT

START   FINISH

PURPOSE: To improve change of direction and lateral speed.

PERFORMANCE: Stand on a sturdy box at least 12 inches high (start). Step off the box (don't jump) and land so that both feet hit the ground at the same time. Immediately sprint several yards to the right or left (finish). Repeat for the required number of repetitions.

POINTERS: You can also perform this exercise with a partner who stands in front of you and points to the direction you should run.

HEXAGON DRILL

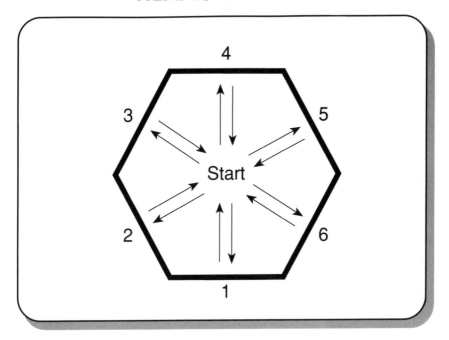

PURPOSE: To improve foot speed and general coordination.

PERFORMANCE: Stand in the middle of the hexagon, feet shoulder-width apart. Jump in the directions shown with feet together. Repeat for the required number of repetitions. As you progress, you will be able to perform this exercise on one leg.

POINTERS: Each side of the hexagon should be 24 inches long.

JUMP AND REACH

PURPOSE: To develop total body power and jumping ability.

PERFORMANCE: Stand with your feet shoulder-width apart. Jump as high as possible while reaching upward with your arms extended. Repeat for the required number of repetitions.

To perform this exercise with a medicine ball, place the ball in your hands, jump and extend your arms overhead as high as possible without releasing the ball.

POINTERS: It helps to have a target to jump for, such as a basketball net, when performing this exercise.

JUMP OVER BARRIER (SIDE)

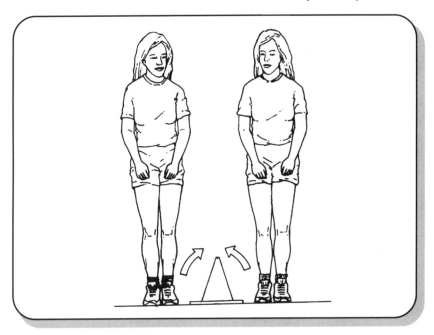

PURPOSE: To develop quick foot movements and lateral speed.

PERFORMANCE: Place a small cone on the ground so that one side of your body is facing the object. Place your feet together. Keeping your knees flexed throughout the exercise, jump back and forth over the object as shown for the required number of repetitions.

POINTERS: This exercise should be performed on a *giving* surface, such as grass. Land with flat feet—not on your toes. Good footwear, such as a cross-training shoe, is also recommended.

JUMP TO BOX

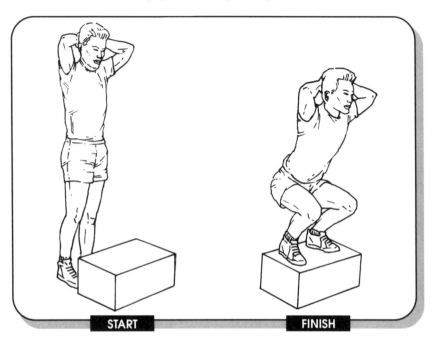

START   **FINISH**

Purpose:
To develop lower body power.

Performance:
Stand 12 to 18 inches in front of a sturdy box, 12 to 24 inches high. Spread your legs about 6 inches apart and place your hands behind your head (start). Jump as high as possible and land on the box. You should finish with your entire foot in contact with the box—*do not land on your toes!* Step down off the box and repeat for the required number of repetitions.

Pointers:
Land softly, making as little noise as possible when landing on the box. Good footwear, such as a cross-training shoe, is recommended.

LATERAL CONE HOPS

PURPOSE: To develop single leg strength and lateral quickness.

PERFORMANCE: Line up five cones, spaced 2 to 3 feet apart as shown. Stand sideways to the far right cone, balancing on your outside leg. Jump sideways between the cones, landing on both feet until you jump over the last cone. On the last cone land on the outside foot and immediately repeat the exercise in the other direction.

POINTERS: Use small cones when you first perform this exercise. Wear sturdy footwear, such as a cross-training shoe, and perform the exercise on a giving surface, such as grass.

PUSH-UP WITH CLAP

PURPOSE: To develop upper body strength and power.

PERFORMANCE: Lie facedown in the push-up position, arms extended. Perform a push-up vigorously, clapping your hands at the top. Repeat in a rhythmical manner for the recommended number of repetitions.

POINTERS: Maintain good posture by keeping your torso rigid throughout the exercise.

SIDE-TO-SIDE BOX SHUFFLE

PURPOSE: To develop anaerobic (short-term) endurance and lateral quickness.

PERFORMANCE: Stand beside a sturdy box, 12 to 18 inches high. Place your left foot on the box. Push off with both legs, clear the box by 1 to 6 inches (your leap is slightly vertical as well as horizontal), and land so that your right foot is on the box and your left foot is on the floor. Continue shuffling back and forth in this manner as fast as you can for 30 seconds.

POINTERS: Use your arms vigorously during this exercise. Land with your feet flat, not on your toes.

SINGLE LEG PUSH-OFF

START   **FINISH**

PURPOSE: To develop anaerobic (short-term) endurance and lower body power.

PERFORMANCE: Place one foot on a sturdy box, 12 to 18 inches high (start). Push off with your forward leg, jumping as high as possible, and land softly on the same leg with balls and front of your foot making contact with the surface of the box. Repeat for the required number of repetitions and switch to the other leg.

POINTERS: Use your arms vigorously during this exercise.

SPLIT SQUAT JUMP

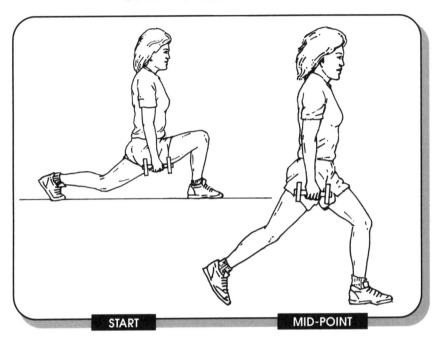

START   MID-POINT

PURPOSE: To develop lower body power and hip flexibility.

PERFORMANCE: Hold a dumbbell in each hand and assume the split position shown (start). Jump as high as possible, splitting your legs as you do (mid-point). Land in the split position. Continue in this manner for the required number of repetitions, jumping in a smooth, rhythmical manner.

POINTERS: Wear sturdy footwear, such as a cross-training shoe, and jump on a giving surface, such as grass.

30-60-90 BOX DRILL

PURPOSE:

To develop anaerobic (short-term) endurance and lateral quickness.

PERFORMANCE:

Stand at the side of a 6- to 12-inch high box with feet shoulder-width apart. Jump onto the box. Land softly on it with both feet. Jump to the ground on the other side. Then jump back onto the box. Continue to jump across the top of the box for the allotted time (30, 60, or 90 seconds as prescribed by the Power Tennis Training workouts presented in Part II of the book). Each time you touch the top of the box counts as 1 repetition. Jump at a rate of 1 repetition per second.

POINTERS:

Use your arms vigorously during this exercise. Also, because this exercise can last up to 90 seconds and is therefore very taxing, it's important to concentrate on technique to avoid tripping or falling.

● Medicine Ball Exercises

Many tennis-specific exercises can be performed with medicine balls. These balls are available in a variety of materials and are generally covered with leather, rubber, or polyurethane. Another popular medicine ball is called a plyo-ball, a soft, loosely packed ball that bounces only slightly and is easy to catch. Because medicine balls are available in a variety of weights, they can accommodate the strength level of any athlete.

In the Power Tennis Training workouts I do not prescribe exact weights for each exercise because, with medicine ball training, it's best to use a variety of weights to stimulate continual adaptations. Generally speaking, however, women will use 4- to 8-pound balls and men will use 8- to 12-pound balls for most exercises. Use lighter weights on one-arm exercises or those that apply to a single muscle group.

BENCH STEP-UP AND PRESS

START   FINISH

PURPOSE:

To strengthen the front and rear thigh muscles (with minimal stress on the lower back) and the shoulders and triceps muscles.

PERFORMANCE:

Stand in front of a box, 12 to 18 inches high. Hold a medicine ball on your chest. Place your weaker leg on the box, keeping the rear foot as close as possible to the box (start). Straighten you front leg, lift yourself up onto the box, and press the weight overhead (finish). Repeat for the required number of repetitions.

POINTERS:

Always keep the rear knee slightly bent during the exercise to improve balance. Perform this exercise slowly at first to perfect your technique.

DROP PASS

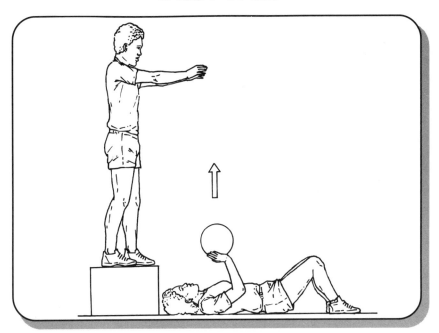

PURPOSE: To develop upper body power.

PERFORMANCE: Lie faceup on the ground with your arms outstretched and hands placed as shown. A partner stands behind your head on a sturdy box at least 12 inches high. Your partner drops the ball onto your hands and you immediately throw the ball (a chest pass) back to your partner. Repeat for the required number of repetitions.

POINTERS: If a partner is not available, you can perform this exercise by yourself, throwing the ball up and catching it.

KNEELING SIDE THROW

PURPOSE:

To develop the muscles on the sides of the waist and upper body power.

PERFORMANCE:

Kneel on the floor facing a partner. Grasp a medicine ball with both hands and twist to one side, following the ball with your eyes as you do. After you have cocked yourself in position, twist your upper body and arms back toward your partner and throw the ball to your partner as shown. Perform the required number of repetitions and repeat for the other side.

POINTERS:

You can perform this exercise with your partner acting as a catcher and a thrower. When first performing this movement, use a light ball (4 to 6 pounds) as this exercise is more stressful than it appears.

OVERHEAD THROW

PURPOSE: To develop upper body power.

PERFORMANCE: Grasp a medicine ball in both hands, palms facing each other. Have a partner stand about 10 feet in front of you to serve as a catcher. Lift the ball overhead and behind you, bending your arms slightly in the cocked position. Take a step while throwing the ball overhead to your partner. Repeat for the required number of repetitions.

POINTERS: If a partner is not available, you can perform this exercise by throwing the ball against a wall.

PULLOVER TOSS

10
Feet

PURPOSE: To develop upper body strength and power.

PERFORMANCE: Lie faceup on the floor with your arms extended behind you. Hold a medicine ball with your hands facing each other. Have a partner stand about 10 feet in front of you to serve as a catcher.

Pull the ball overhead and to your chest while moving into a sitting position. Perform a chest pass to your partner. Remain in the upright position to catch the toss-back from your partner. Repeat for the required number of repetitions.

POINTERS: To make the exercise harder, have your partner stand further back.

CHAPTER 5

COURT DRILLS

Court drills improve your agility and endurance. The 10 drills covered in this chapter are designed to supplement the Power Tennis Training program workouts described in Part II. You will run drills 3 times a week for 12 weeks. Twice a week you will perform 3 drills and once a week you will perform 4 drills. This way, you will run all 10 drills each week but never the same drill twice in the same week. You will also be directed to modify these drills over the 12-week cycle so that your training won't become stale.

Once you have completed the 12-week program during your off-season training, you can pick and choose the drills that will be most helpful to you during your heavy tournament schedule. (It's better to concentrate more on resistance training during the competitive season.) Run your drills after you have completed your day's matches. If the day's match turns out to be tough, you won't want to have used up energy before the match.

🎾 The Court Drills

Each court drill contains an exercise prescription with the following terms:

- Reps (how many times you will perform each drill)
- Time (how long you perform the drill in a single rep—expressed in seconds or minutes)
- Rest (how much rest time you should take after each rep—also expressed in either seconds or minutes)

Look at the sample exercise prescription in Figure 5.1.

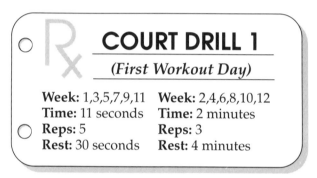

Figure 5.1   Exercise prescription for Court Drill 1.

From this example you know that on the 6th week you will perform this drill for three reps. It will take 2 minutes to complete each rep. And you will rest for 4 minutes after each rep.

The following pages map out each of the court drills, using the following key:

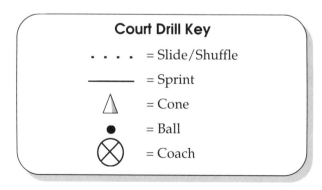

Generally, these drills call for you to run or shuffle back to positions on the court marked by cones. You may run these drills alone if you can accurately track your timing. If you sense it helps, you may want to carry a racquet when you run these, and, of course, you should wear court shoes. Drills 7 and 8 require that a coach or a partner toss you balls to catch.

I've designed these drill progressions so that each drill will emphasize speed on some days and on other days, endurance. The exceptions are Drills 5 and 6, which only emphasize speed. To achieve the appropriate training effect, you must perform each drill exactly as I've prescribed, with the appropriate number of reps at the correct speed and with the recommended rest intervals.

COURT DRILL 1

(First Workout Day)

Week: 1,3,5,7,9,11	**Week:** 2,4,6,8,10,12
Time: 11 seconds	**Time:** 2 minutes
Reps: 5	**Reps:** 3
Rest: 30 seconds	**Rest:** 4 minutes

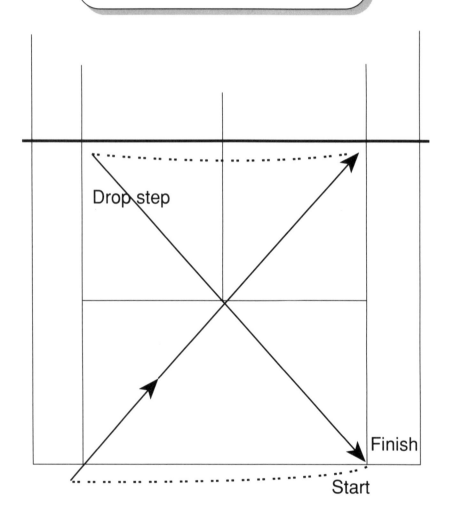

COURT DRILL 2

(First Workout Day)

Week: 1,3,5,7,9,11   **Week:** 2,4,6,8,10,12
Time: 5 seconds   **Time:** 7 seconds
Reps: 8   **Reps:** 10
Rest: 20 seconds   **Rest:** 30 seconds

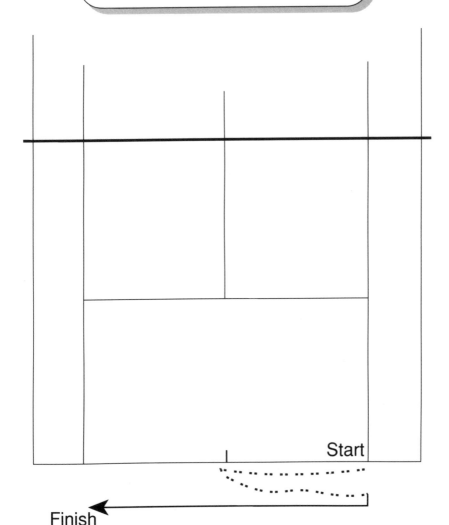

COURT DRILL 3

(First Workout Day)

Week: 1,3,5,7,9,11   **Week:** 2,4,6,8,10,12
Time: 14 seconds   **Time:** 30 seconds
Reps: 4   **Reps:** 3
Rest: 45 seconds   **Rest:** 4 minutes

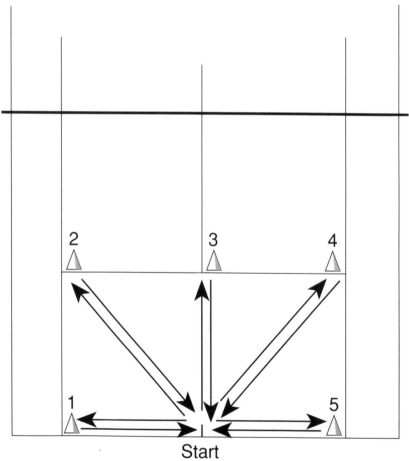

Start
Finish

COURT DRILL 4
(Second Workout Day)

Week: 1,3,5,7,9,11   **Week:** 2,4,6,8,10,12
Time: 1 minute   **Time:** 90 seconds
Reps: 3   **Reps:** 5
Rest: 60 seconds   **Rest:** 90 seconds

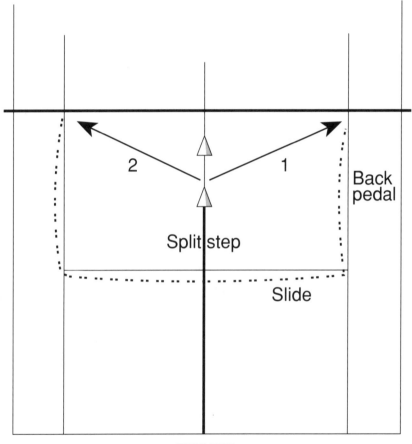

COURT DRILL 5

(Second Workout Day)

Week: All Weeks
Time: 3 seconds
Reps: 10
Rest: 15 seconds

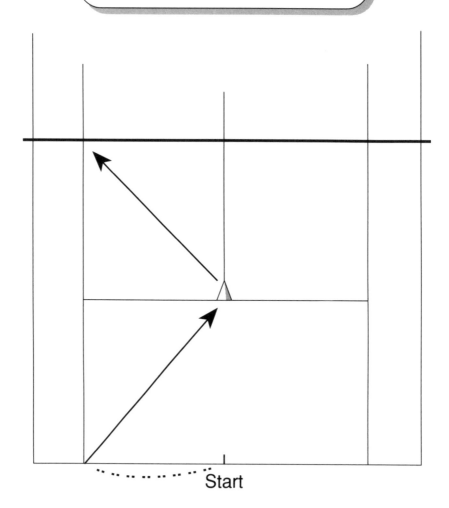

Start

COURT DRILL 6

(Second Workout Day)

Week: All Weeks
Time: 3 seconds
Reps: 10
Rest: 15 seconds

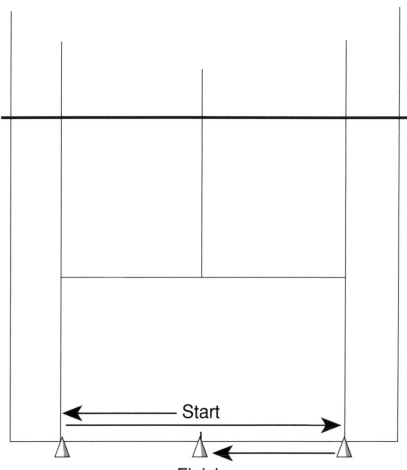

COURT DRILL 7
(Third Workout Day)

Week: 1,3,5,7,9,11   **Week:** 2,4,6,8,10,12
Time: 10 seconds   **Time:** 30 seconds
Reps: 10   **Reps:** 5
Rest: 30 seconds **Rest:** 1 minute

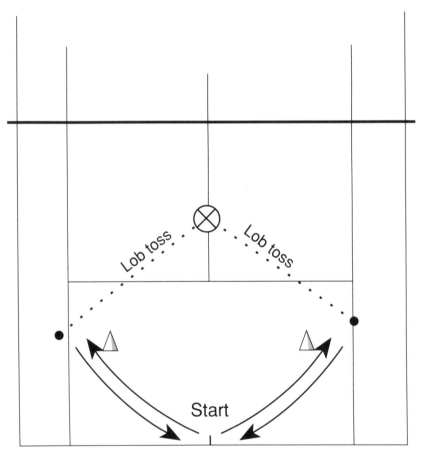

COURT DRILL 8

(Third Workout Day)

Week: All Weeks
Time: 2 seconds
Reps: 10
Rest: 10 seconds

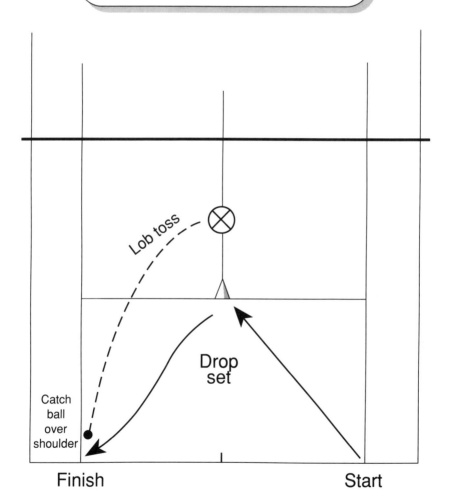

COURT DRILL 9

(Third Workout Day)

Week: 1,3,5,7,9,11	**Week:** 2,4,6,8,10,12
Time: 30 seconds	**Time:** 40 seconds
Reps: 5	**Reps:** 6
Rest: 45 seconds	**Rest:** 1 minute

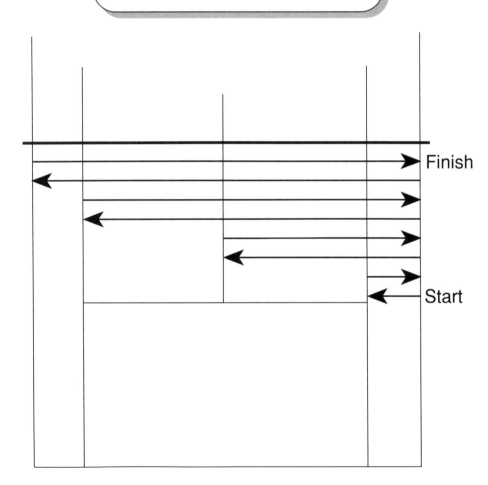

Finish

Start

COURT DRILL 10

(Third Workout Day)

Week: 1,3,5,7,9,11   **Week:** 2,4,6,8,10,12
Time: 20 seconds   **Time:** 90 seconds
Reps: 4   **Reps:** 2
Rest: 60 seconds   **Rest:** 3 minutes

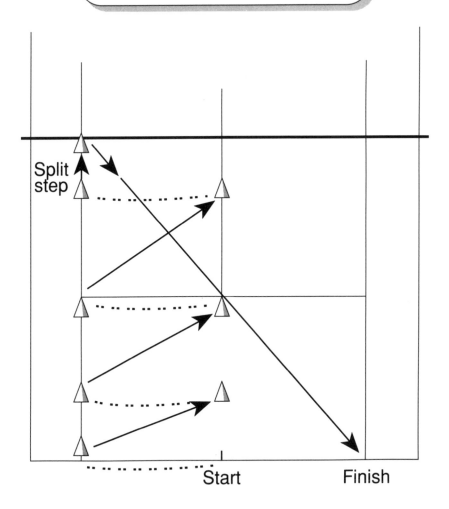

PART · II

POWER TENNIS WORKOUTS

CHAPTER 6

BUILDING BLOCKS APPROACH TO WORKOUTS

The complete Power Tennis Training program lasts 12 weeks, divided among three 4-week training blocks. For best results, perform the training phases in this order:

Block 1: Strength-endurance
Block 2: Strength
Block 3: Power

Your body adapts to a single workout program quickly, and many tennis players become frustrated with off-court conditioning because their workouts are monotonous. That's why, as your body adapts to a specific workout in the Power Tennis Training conditioning system, the workout changes. Table 6.1 charts the variety of training methods used in this program.

Why not perform all of these training methods from the start? Because it takes time to develop the necessary conditioning for the more advanced training methods, like the power complexes in Block 3. This is true with many other sports; take distance running, for example. Elite runners often run several times a day, and it's not unusual for them to

Table 6.1 Summary of Training Methods			
TRAINING METHOD	**BLOCK 1**	**BLOCK 2**	**BLOCK 3**
Abdominal circuit*	Yes	Yes	Yes
Complex*	Yes	Yes	No
Court drills	Yes	Yes	Yes
Medicine ball	Yes	Yes	Yes
Power complex	No	No	Yes
Power circuit	No	No	Yes
Plyometrics	Yes	Yes	Yes
Weight training (conventional)	Yes	Yes	Yes
Weight training circuit	Yes	Yes	Yes
Wrist/forearm circuit	Yes	Yes	Yes

*Note. A complex is a type of set in which two exercises are performed alternately (instead of the conventional method of performing all the sets of one exercise before moving on to the next exercise). A circuit is a set in which several exercises are performed in sequence.

run more than 100 miles a week. But of course they certainly didn't start their training with 100-mile weeks; yet once these athletes reach such a high level of conditioning, only workouts of this intensity will push them sufficiently.

Chapters 7 through 9 present workout tables for each block of the program. Because you may want to repeat this program again and again, I suggest you photocopy the tables in this part of the book. I've left room for you to keep track of your weights and reps. Always follow the workouts in the order and manner they are prescribed in the tables. Skipping workouts will retard your progress, but doubling up could cause overtraining, which will also retard your progress. If you're not feeling 100% or are rushed for time, reduce the number of sets, but still *go heavy!*

CHAPTER 7

BLOCK 1: STRENGTH-ENDURANCE WORKOUTS

You should perform Block 1 workouts at least 2, but preferably 3, days a week for the first 4 weeks of the Power Tennis Training program. If you train 3 days a week, the workouts for Days 1 and 3 are the same.

The first (and third) workout of each week consists of nine parts, including the warm-up. The parts should be performed in this order:

1. Standard warm-up
2. Plyometrics and medicine ball
3. Complex 1*
4. Complex 2
5. Weight training circuit 1*
6. Weight training circuit 2
7. Weight training (conventional method)
8. Abdominal circuit
9. Wrist-forearm circuit

*Note: A **complex** is a type of set in which two exercises are performed alternately (instead of the conventional method of performing all the sets of one exercise before moving to the next exercise). A **circuit** is a set in which several exercises are performed in sequence.

The second workout of each week likewise consists of nine parts, including the warm-up, to be performed in this order:

1. Standard warm-up
2. Plyometrics and medicine ball
3. Complex 1
4. Complex 2
5. Weight training circuit 1
6. Weight training circuit 2
7. Weight training (conventional method)
8. Abdominal circuit
9. Wrist-forearm circuit

Although these parts have the same names as the parts of the first workout, the content of some parts is different.

After every workout, you need to perform 5 to 10 minutes of the postworkout stretches from chapter 2.

Also, you will supplement your Block 1 workouts (preferably on days you are resting from the workouts described in this chapter) by running the court drills for Weeks 1 through 4 of the program.

Block 1
Strength and endurance workouts

Duration: 4 weeks

Workouts
3 per week using
training components
from Part I

Supplementary Work
Weeks 1-4 of
court drill program
from chapter 5

BLOCK 1: DAYS 1 & 3

Workout   1   2   3   4   5   6   7   8

Note: Unless otherwise stated, rest 1 min after every set. r = reps; s = sets; sec = seconds

1. Standard warm-up

2. Plyometrics and medicine ball

Lateral cone hops: 9 jumps × 2s
Side-to-side box shuffle: 10r × 3s
Single leg push-off: 10(30 sec)r × 3s
Overhead throw: 15r × 2s
  Weight: _____ _____ _____ _____ _____ _____ _____ _____
Kneeling side throw: 15r × 2s
  Weight: _____ _____ _____ _____ _____ _____ _____ _____
Hexagon drill: 3 rotations × 2s

3. Complex 1 (2s)

Push press: 12r Tempo: max speed
  Weight: _____ _____ _____ _____ _____ _____ _____ _____
Jump to box: 10r
                    Rest 2-3 min after each set

4. Complex 2 (2s)

Leg press: 10r Up at moderate speed, no pause, down in 4 sec
  Weight: _____ _____ _____ _____ _____ _____ _____ _____
                    Split squat jump: 10r
Rest 2-3 min after each set

5. Weight training circuit 1 (2s)

Back squat: 10r Down in 4 sec, no pause, up at moderate speed
  Weight: _____ _____ _____ _____ _____ _____ _____ _____
Front lunge: 6r (each leg) Down in 4 sec, no pause, up at moderate speed
  Weight: _____ _____ _____ _____ _____ _____ _____ _____
Side lunge: 6r (each leg) Down in 4 sec, no pause, up at moderate speed
  Weight: _____ _____ _____ _____ _____ _____ _____ _____
Calf raise (machine): 20r Up at moderate speed, no pause, down in 4 sec
  Weight: _____ _____ _____ _____ _____ _____ _____ _____
                    Rest 2-3 min after each set

Workout   1   2   3   4   5   6   7   8

6. Weight training circuit 2 (2s)

Upright row: 10r Up at moderate speed, no pause, down in 4 sec

Weight: ____ ____ ____ ____ ____ ____ ____ ____

Seated row: 10r Up at moderate speed, no pause, down in 4 sec

Weight: ____ ____ ____ ____ ____ ____ ____ ____

Front pulldown: 10r Down at moderate speed, no pause, up in 4 sec

Weight: ____ ____ ____ ____ ____ ____ ____ ____

Pullover: 10r Down in 4 sec, no pause, up at moderate speed

Weight: ____ ____ ____ ____ ____ ____ ____ ____

Rest 2-3 min after each set

7. Weight training (conventional method)

Back extension: 10r × 2s Up at moderate speed, no pause, down in 4 sec

Weight: ____ ____ ____ ____ ____ ____ ____ ____

Rest 2-3 min after each set

8. Abdominal circuit (1s)

Knee pull-in: 25r

Russian twist: 10r (each side) Down in 4 sec, no pause, up at moderate speed

Weight: ____ ____ ____ ____ ____ ____ ____ ____

Sit-up with legs raised: 25r

Hip press-up: 15r

9. Wrist-forearm circuit (1s)

Wrist flexion: 20r Moderate speed

Weight: ____ ____ ____ ____ ____ ____ ____ ____

Wrist extension: 20r Moderate speed

Weight: ____ ____ ____ ____ ____ ____ ____ ____

Wrist pronation/supination: 20r Moderate speed

Weight: ____ ____ ____ ____ ____ ____ ____ ____

Wrist ulnar flexion: 20r Moderate speed

Weight: ____ ____ ____ ____ ____ ____ ____ ____

Wrist radial flexion: 20r Moderate speed

Weight: ____ ____ ____ ____ ____ ____ ____ ____

Additional work: Postworkout stretches: 5-10 min

Supplementary court drills: Weeks 1-4 (see chapter 5)

BLOCK 1: DAY 2

Workout　　1　　2　　3　　4

Note: Unless otherwise stated, rest 1 min after every set. r = reps; s = sets; sec = seconds

1. Standard warm-up

2. Plyometrics and medicine ball
Lateral cone hops: 9 jumps × 2s
Side-to-side box shuffle: 10r (30 sec) × 3s
Single leg push-off: 10(30 sec)r × 3s
Overhead throw: 15r × 2s
　Weight: _____ _____ _____ _____
Kneeling side throw: 15r × 2s
　Weight: _____ _____ _____ _____
Hexagon drill: 3 rotations × 2s

3. Complex 1 (2s)
Front squat to push press: 10r Tempo: max speed
　Weight: _____ _____ _____ _____
Jump to box: 12r
　　　　　　　Rest 3-4 min after each set

4. Complex 2 (2s)
Leg press: 10r Up at moderate speed, no pause, down in 4 sec
　Weight: _____ _____ _____ _____
Jump and reach: 12r
　　　　　　　Rest 2-3 min after each set

5. Weight training circuit 1 (2s)
Walking lunge: 12r Moderate speed
　Weight: _____ _____ _____ _____
Bench step-up: 10r Up at moderate speed, no pause, down in 4 sec
　Weight: _____ _____ _____ _____
Leg curl (facedown): 10r Up at moderate speed, no pause, down in 4 sec
　Weight: _____ _____ _____ _____
Calf raise (seated): 20r Up at moderate speed, no pause, down in 4 sec
　Weight: _____ _____ _____ _____
　　　　　　　Rest 2-3 min after each set

Workout   1   2   3   4

6. Weight training circuit 2

Bench press: 10r Down in 4 sec, no pause, up at moderate speed

Weight: _____ _____ _____ _____

Front pulldown: 10r Down at moderate speed, no pause, up in 4 sec

Weight: _____ _____ _____ _____

Pec dec: 10r Up at moderate speed, no pause, down in 4 sec

Weight: _____ _____ _____ _____

Dumbbell row: 10r Up at moderate speed, no pause, down in 4 sec

Weight: _____ _____ _____ _____

Rest 2-3 min after each set

7. Weight training (conventional method)

Back extension: 10r × 2s Up at moderate speed, no pause, down in 4 sec

Weight: _____ _____ _____ _____

Rest 2-3 min after each set

8. Abdominal circuit (1s)

Knee pull-in: 25r

Russian twist: 10r (each side) Down in 4 sec, no pause, up at moderate speed

Weight: _____ _____ _____ _____

Sit-up with legs raised: 25r

Hip press-up: 15r

9. Wrist-forearm circuit (1s)

Wrist flexion: 20r Moderate speed

Weight: _____ _____ _____ _____

Wrist extension: 20r Moderate speed

Weight: _____ _____ _____ _____

Wrist pronation/supination: 20r Moderate speed

Weight: _____ _____ _____ _____

Wrist ulnar flexion: 20r Moderate speed

Weight: _____ _____ _____ _____

Wrist radial flexion: 20r Moderate speed

Weight: _____ _____ _____ _____

Additional work: Postworkout stretches: 5-10 min

Supplementary court drills: Weeks 1-4 (see chapter 5)

CHAPTER 8

BLOCK 2:
STRENGTH
WORKOUTS

You should perform Block 2 workouts at least 2, but preferably 3, days a week for the first 4 weeks of the Power Tennis Training program. If you train 3 days a week, the workouts for Days 1 and 3 are the same.

The first (and third) workout of each week consists of eight parts, including the warm-up. The parts should be performed in this order:

1. Standard warm-up
2. Complex 1*
3. Complex 2
4. Complex 3
5. Weight training (conventional method)
6. Plyometrics and medicine ball
7. Abdominal circuit*
8. Wrist-forearm circuit

*Note: A **complex** is a type of set in which two exercises are performed alternately (instead of the conventional method of performing all the sets of one exercise before moving to the next exercise). A **circuit** is a set in which several exercises are performed in sequence.

The second workout of each week consists of the following nine parts, including the warm-up, to be performed in this order:

1. Standard warm-up
2. Complex 1
3. Complex 2
4. Weight training circuit 1
5. Weight training circuit 2
6. Plyometrics and medicine ball
7. Weight training (conventional method)
8. Abdominal circuit
9. Wrist-forearm circuit

After every workout, you need to perform 5 to 10 minutes of the postworkout stretches from chapter 2.

Also, you will supplement your Block 2 workouts (preferably on days you are resting from the workouts described in this chapter) by running the court drills for Weeks 5 through 8 of the program.

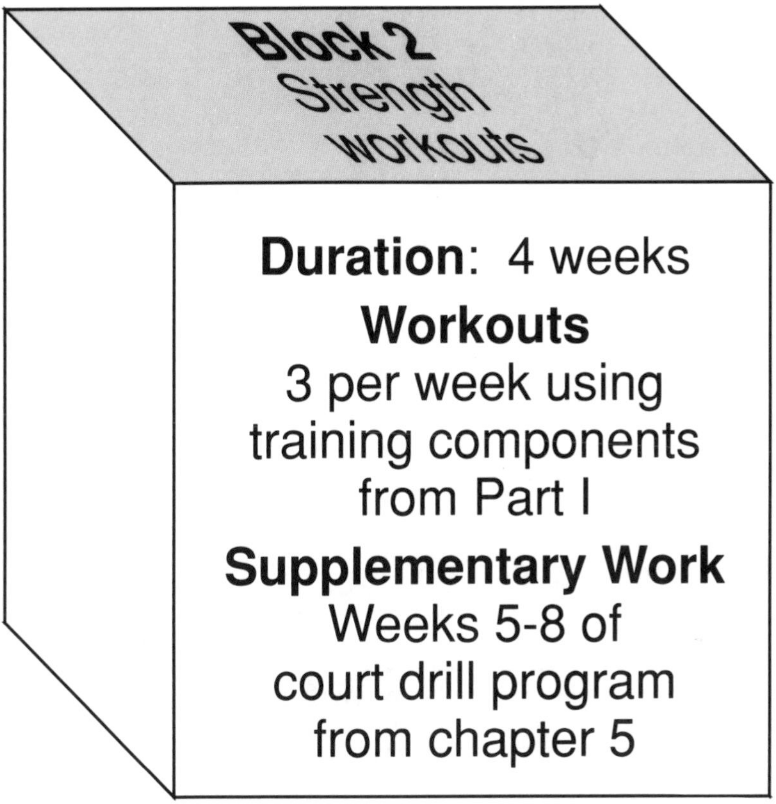

Block 2
Strength
workouts

Duration: 4 weeks

Workouts
3 per week using
training components
from Part I

Supplementary Work
Weeks 5-8 of
court drill program
from chapter 5

BLOCK 2: DAYS 1 & 3

Workout   1   2   3   4   5   6   7   8

Note: *Unless otherwise stated, rest 1 min after every set. r = reps; s = sets; sec = seconds*

1. Standard warm-up

2. Complex 1 (2s)

Front squat to push press: 6r Tempo: max speed

Weight: ____ ____ ____ ____ ____ ____ ____ ____

Dumbbell split jerk: 8r Tempo: max speed

Weight: ____ ____ ____ ____ ____ ____ ____ ____

Rest 2-3 min after each set

3. Complex 2 (2s)

Front lunge: 4r (each leg) Down to 3, pause for 1, up at max speed

Weight: ____ ____ ____ ____ ____ ____ ____ ____

Split squat jump: 8r

Rest 2-3 min after each set

4. Complex 3 (2s)

Bench press: 6r Down in 3 sec, pause for 1 sec, up at max speed

Weight: ____ ____ ____ ____ ____ ____ ____ ____

Push-up with clap (from knees if necessary): 8r

Rest 2-3 min after each set

5. Weight training (conventional method) (2s)

Leg press: 6r Up at max speed, pause for 1 sec, down in 3 sec

Weight: ____ ____ ____ ____ ____ ____ ____ ____

Back extension: 8r Up at max speed, pause for 1 sec, down in 3 sec

Weight: ____ ____ ____ ____ ____ ____ ____ ____

Back pulldown: 6r Down at max speed, pause for 1 sec, up in 3 sec

Weight: ____ ____ ____ ____ ____ ____ ____ ____

Front raise (dumbbells): 6r Up at max speed, pause for 1 sec, down in 3 sec

Weight: ____ ____ ____ ____ ____ ____ ____ ____

External shoulder rotation (on side): 8r Moderate speed

Weight: ____ ____ ____ ____ ____ ____ ____ ____

Rest 2-3 min after each set

Workout	1	2	3	4	5	6	7	8

6. Plyometrics and medicine ball

Depth jump with lateral movement: 8r × 2s
30-60-90 box drill (30 sec): 2s
Pullover toss: 15r × 3s

   Weight: _____ _____ _____ _____ _____ _____ _____ _____
Lateral cone hops: 9 jumps × 3s
Kneeling side throw: 15r × 2s

   Weight: _____ _____ _____ _____ _____ _____ _____ _____
Jump to box: 8r × 2s

7. Abdominal circuit (1s)

Hip rotation: 10r (each direction)
Hip roll: 15r
Knee pull-in: 15r
Side sit-up: 12r
Russian twist: 10r (each side) Down in 3 sec, pause for 1 sec, up at max speed

   Weight: _____ _____ _____ _____ _____ _____ _____ _____
Rest 2-3 min after each set

8. Wrist-forearm circuit (1s)

Wrist flexion: 20r Moderate speed

   Weight: _____ _____ _____ _____ _____ _____ _____ _____
Wrist extension: 20r Moderate speed

   Weight: _____ _____ _____ _____ _____ _____ _____ _____
Wrist pronation/supination: 20r Moderate speed

   Weight: _____ _____ _____ _____ _____ _____ _____ _____
Wrist ulnar flexion: 20r Moderate speed

   Weight: _____ _____ _____ _____ _____ _____ _____ _____
Wrist radial flexion: 20r Moderate speed

   Weight: _____ _____ _____ _____ _____ _____ _____ _____

Additional work: Postworkout stretches: 5-10 min
Supplementary court drills: Weeks 5-8 (see chapter 5)

BLOCK 2: DAY 2

Workout   1   2   3   4

Note: Unless otherwise stated, rest 1 min after every set. r = reps; s = sets; sec = seconds

1. Standard warm-up

2. Complex 1 (2s)

Dumbbell split jerk: 5r Tempo: max speed

   Weight: _____ _____ _____ _____ _____ _____ _____

Bench step-up and press: 8r

   Weight: _____ _____ _____ _____ _____ _____ _____

Rest 2-3 min after each set

3. Complex 2 (2s)

Leg press: 6r Down in 3 sec, pause for 1 sec, up at max speed

   Weight: _____ _____ _____ _____ _____ _____ _____

Hexagon drill: 3 rotations

Rest 2-3 min after each set

4. Weight training circuit 1 (2s)

Front lunge: 5r (each leg) Down in 3 sec, pause for 1 sec, up at max speed

   Weight: _____ _____ _____ _____ _____ _____ _____

45-degree lunge: 5r (each leg) Down in 3 sec, pause for 1 sec, up at max speed

   Weight: _____ _____ _____ _____ _____ _____ _____

Side lunge: 5r (each leg) Down in 3 sec, pause for 1 sec, up at max speed

   Weight: _____ _____ _____ _____ _____ _____ _____

Cross-over lunge: 5r (each leg) Down in 3 sec, pause for 1 sec, up at max speed

   Weight: _____ _____ _____ _____ _____ _____ _____

Rest 2-3 min after each set

5. Weight training circuit 2 (2s)

Bench press: 6r Down in 3 sec, pause for 1 sec, up at max speed

   Weight: _____ _____ _____ _____ _____ _____ _____

Upright row: 6r Up at max speed, pause for 1 sec, up at max speed

   Weight: _____ _____ _____ _____ _____ _____ _____

Front pulldown: 6r Down at max speed, pause for 1 sec, up in 3 sec

   Weight: _____ _____ _____ _____ _____ _____ _____

Front raise (dumbbells): 6r Up at max speed, pause for 1 sec, down in 3 sec

   Weight: _____ _____ _____ _____ _____ _____ _____

Rest 2-3 min after each set

Workout   1   2   3   4

6. Plyometrics and medicine ball

Depth jump with lateral movement: 8r × 2s
Split squat jump: 10r × 2s
30-60-90 box drill (30 sec): 2s
Pullover toss: 15r × 3s

Weight: _____ _____ _____ _____
Lateral cone hops: 9 jumps × 3s
Kneeling side throw: 15r × 2s

Weight: _____ _____ _____ _____
Jump to box: 8r × 3s

7. Weight training (conventional method)

Back extension: 10r × 2s Up at moderate speed, no pause, down in 3 sec

Weight: _____ _____ _____ _____
Rest 2-3 min after each set

8. Abdominal circuit (1s)

Hip rotation: 10r (each direction)
Hip roll: 15r
Knee pull-in: 15r
Side sit-up: 12r
Russian twist: 10r (each side) Down in 3 sec, pause for 1 sec, up at max speed

Weight: _____ _____ _____ _____
Bicycle: 30 sec

9. Wrist-forearm circuit (1s)

Wrist flexion: 20r Moderate speed

Weight: _____ _____ _____ _____
Wrist extension: 20r Moderate speed

Weight: _____ _____ _____ _____
Wrist pronation/supination: 20r Moderate speed

Weight: _____ _____ _____ _____
Wrist ulnar flexion: 20r Moderate speed

Weight: _____ _____ _____ _____
Wrist radial flexion: 20r Moderate speed

Weight: _____ _____ _____ _____

Additional work: Postworkout stretches: 5-10 min
Supplementary court drills: Weeks 5-8 (see chapter 5)

CHAPTER
9

BLOCK 3: POWER WORKOUTS

You should perform Block 3 workouts at least 2, but preferably 3, days a week for the first 4 weeks of the Power Tennis Training program. If you train 3 days a week, the workouts for Days 1 and 3 are the same.

The first (and third) workout of each week consists of eight parts, including the warm-up. The parts should be performed in this order:

1. Standard warm-up
2. Power circuit 1*
3. Power circuit 2
4. Power circuit 3
5. Power complex*
6. Weight training (conventional method)
7. Abdominal circuit
8. Wrist-forearm circuit

*Note: A **complex** is a type of set in which two exercises are performed alternately (instead of the conventional method of performing all the sets of one exercise before moving to the next exercise). A **circuit** is a set in which several exercises are performed in sequence.

The second workout of each week consists of the following eight parts, including the warm-up. These parts, and the order they should be performed, are as follows:

1. Standard warm-up
2. Power complex 1
3. Power circuit 1
4. Power complex 2
5. Weight training circuit
6. Weight training (conventional method)
7. Abdominal circuit
8. Wrist-forearm circuit

After each workout, you need to perform 5 to 10 minutes of the postworkout stretches from chapter 2.

Also, you will supplement your Block 3 workouts (preferably on days you are resting from the workouts described in this chapter) by running the court drills for Weeks 9 through 12 of the program.

Block 3
Power
workouts

Duration: 4 weeks

Workouts
3 per week using
training components
from Part I

Supplementary Work
Weeks 9-12 of
court drill program
from chapter 5

BLOCK 3: DAYS 1 & 3

Workout   1   2   3   4   5   6   7   8

Note: Unless otherwise stated, rest 1 min after every set. r = reps; s = sets; sec = seconds

1. Standard warm-up

2. Power circuit 1 (2s)

Front squat to push press: 5r Tempo: max speed

Weight: _____ _____ _____ _____ _____ _____ _____ _____

Dumbbell split jerk: 6r Tempo: max speed

Weight: _____ _____ _____ _____ _____ _____ _____ _____

Rest 2-3 min after each set

3. Power circuit 2 (2s)

Back squat: 5r Down in 1 sec, no pause, up at max speed

Weight: _____ _____ _____ _____ _____ _____ _____ _____

Split squat jump: 10r

Jump over barrier (side): 12r

Rest 3-4 min after each set

4. Power circuit 3 (2s)

Incline press (barbell): 5r Down in 2 sec, no pause, up at max speed

Weight: _____ _____ _____ _____ _____ _____ _____ _____

Push-up with clap (from knees if necessary): 10r

Drop pass: 12r

Rest 2-3 min after each set

5. Power complex (2s)

Pullover: 5r Down in 3 sec, no pause, up at max speed

Weight: _____ _____ _____ _____ _____ _____ _____ _____

Pullover toss: 8r

Weight: _____ _____ _____ _____ _____ _____ _____ _____

Rest 2-3 min after each set

Workout	1	2	3	4	5	6	7	8

6. Weight training (conventional method) (2s)

Side lunge: 4r (each side) Down in 2 sec, no pause, up at max speed

Weight: _____ _____ _____ _____ _____ _____ _____ _____

Back pulldown: 5r Down at max speed, no pause, up in 2 sec

Weight: _____ _____ _____ _____ _____ _____ _____ _____

Glute-ham raise: 5r Up at max speed, no pause, down in 2 sec

Weight: _____ _____ _____ _____ _____ _____ _____ _____

Rest 2-3 min after each set

7. Abdominal circuit (2s)

Knee pull-in: 15r
Hip press-up: 20r
Bicycle: 30r
Side sit-up: 12r

8. Wrist-forearm circuit (1s)

Wrist flexion: 20r Moderate speed

Weight: _____ _____ _____ _____ _____ _____ _____ _____

Wrist extension: 20r Moderate speed

Weight: _____ _____ _____ _____ _____ _____ _____ _____

Wrist pronation/supination: 20r Moderate speed

Weight: _____ _____ _____ _____ _____ _____ _____ _____

Wrist ulnar flexion: 20r Moderate speed

Weight: _____ _____ _____ _____ _____ _____ _____ _____

Wrist radial flexion: 20r Moderate speed

Weight: _____ _____ _____ _____ _____ _____ _____ _____

Additional work: Postworkout stretches: 5-10 min
Supplementary court drills: Weeks 9-12 (see chapter 5)

BLOCK 3: DAY 2

Workout   1   2   3   4

Note: Unless otherwise stated, rest 1 min after every set. r = reps; s = sets; sec = seconds

1. Standard warm-up

2. Power complex 1 (3s)

Bench step-up: 5r Tempo: Up at max speed, no pause, down in 2 sec

Weight: _____ _____ _____ _____

Jump to box: 10r

Rest 2-3 min after each set

3. Power complex 2 (3s)

Front lunge: 5r (each leg) Down in 2 sec, no pause, up at max speed

Weight: _____ _____ _____ _____

Split squat jump: 10r

Rest 2-3 min after each set

4. Power complex 3 (3s)

Pullover and press: 5r

Weight: _____ _____ _____ _____

Pullover toss: 15r

Weight: _____ _____ _____ _____

Rest 2-3 min after each set

5. Weight training circuit (3s)

Back squat: 5r Down in 2 sec, no pause, up at max speed

Weight: _____ _____ _____ _____

Seated row: 5r Up at max speed, no pause, down in 2 sec

Weight: _____ _____ _____ _____

Calf raise (single leg): 12r Up at max speed, no pause, down in 2 sec

Weight: _____ _____ _____ _____

30-60-90 box drill (Week 1 = 30 sec; Week 2 = 60 sec; Weeks 3-4 = 90 sec)

Rest 2-3 min after each set

Workout   1   2   3   4

6. Weight training (conventional method) (3s)

External shoulder rotation (seated): 10r Moderate speed

Weight: ____   ____   ____   ____

External shoulder rotation (on side): 10r Moderate speed

Weight: ____   ____   ____   ____

7. Abdominal circuit (2s)

Knee pull-in: 15r

Hip press-up: 20r

Bicycle: 30r

Side sit-up: 12r

8. Wrist-forearm circuit (1s)

Wrist flexion: 20r Moderate speed

Weight: ____   ____   ____   ____

Wrist extension: 20r Moderate speed

Weight: ____   ____   ____   ____

Wrist pronation/supination: 20r Moderate speed

Weight: ____   ____   ____   ____

Wrist ulnar flexion: 20r Moderate speed

Weight: ____   ____   ____   ____

Wrist radial flexion: 20r Moderate speed

Weight: ____   ____   ____   ____

Additional work: Postworkout stretches: 5-10 min

Supplementary court drills: Weeks 9-12 (see chapter 5)

APPENDIX

FITNESS TESTING WORKSHEET

Fitness testing helps you monitor the effectiveness of your training program and tells you which aspects of conditioning you need to improve. For example, if you perform poorly on the 90-second box drill, you may need to perform additional endurance work. Continually testing and acting upon the results of testing will help prevent any weak links from developing in your game.

When deciding on a field (nonweightlifting) test, you should select from tests that are simple, require no special equipment, and can be performed in a few minutes. Here are a few samples:

- the hexagon drill (testing agility and footspeed),
- a seated machine ball toss (testing upper body power),
- a standing long jump (testing lower body power),
- a 90-second box drill (testing anaerobic endurance), and
- a 10-yard sprint (testing starting speed).

It's also important to keep records on how much you can lift. The traditional method of recording how much you can lift is to have you lift the most you can for a single repetition. This tells you your one-repetition maximum (1RM). Fortunately, it's not necessary to perform 1RM lifts to determine your maximum effort. Using your completed workout sheets, you can predict your maximum effort based on submaximum efforts. One formula to help you determine a 1RM is this:

Weight lifted × coefficient of repetitions = 1RM

Table A.1 charts the coefficient of repetitions that will allow you to figure your maximum effort (1RM). For example, if you can bench press 100 pounds for 10 reps, you would perform the following calculation:

100 (weight) × 1.2 (coefficient from Table A.1) =
120 pounds maximum effort (1RM)

Table A.1 Predicting Maximums Based on Submaximum Efforts	
NUMBER OF REPS POSSIBLE WITH A SPECIFIC WEIGHT	**COEFFICIENT TO MULTIPLY FOR 1 RM**
1 rep	1.00
2 reps	1.04
3 reps	1.06
4 reps	1.08
5 reps	1.10
6 reps	1.12
7 reps	1.14
8 reps	1.16
9 reps	1.18
10 reps	1.20
Weight lifted × coefficient of repetitions = maximum effort (1RM)	

The following pages contain a testing worksheet that you can use to record your goals and testing results and a sample of a completed testing form. You can test as frequently as you desire (the sample testing form is for someone who tests once a month), but I recommend you test at least at the end of each complete Power Tennis Training program (once every 3 months).

Table A.2 Sample Sports Fitness Testing Sheet

NAME: _John Doe_

LEGEND: G = Goal
A = Achieved

DESCRIPTION	Date: 5/22		Date: 8/23		Date: 11/24		Date: 12/22		Date: 1/20	
	G	A	G	A	G	A	G	A	G	A
① Hexagon drill (30 sec)	7	6	7	7	8	7	8	7	8	8
② Seated medicine ball toss (8 lbs)	25'	20'	25'	21'	25'	23'	25'	24'	25'	25'
③ Standing long jump	8.06	7	8.06	7.02	8.06	7.07	8.06	8.0	8.06	8.0
④ 90-second box drill (12" box)	70	60	70	72	75	74	75	77	80	77
⑤ 10-yard sprint		1.75	1.82	1.75	1.83	1.75	1.77	1.75	1.78	1.75	1.76
⑥ Body fat percent	18	20	18	18	17	18	17	19	17	17.5
☐										
☐										
☐										
☐										
☐										
☐										
☐										
☐										
☐										
☐										
☐										
☐										

Table A.3   Sports Fitness Testing Sheet

NAME: _____

LEGEND: G = Goal
         A = Achieved

DESCRIPTION	Date:		Date:		Date:		Date:		Date:	
	G	A	G	A	G	A	G	A	G	A
❏										
❏										
❏										
❏										
❏										
❏										
❏										
❏										
❏										
❏										
❏										
❏										
❏										
❏										
❏										
❏										
❏										
❏										

EXERCISE INDEX

Arm Circles 23

Back Extension 36

Back Squat 38

Bench Press 40

Bench Step-Up 42

Bench Step-Up and Press 110

Bicycle 85

Calf Raise (Machine) 44

Calf Raise (Seated) 46

Court Drill 1 118

Court Drill 2 119

Court Drill 3 120

Court Drill 4 121

Court Drill 5 122

Court Drill 6 123

Court Drill 7 124

Court Drill 8 125

Court Drill 9 126

Court Drill 10 127

Cross-Over Lunge 47

Depth Jump With Lateral Movement 98

Drop Pass 111

Dumbbell Row 48

Dumbbell Split Jerk 49

External/Internal Rotation (Faceup) 21

External Shoulder Rotation (On Side) 50

External Shoulder Rotation (Seated) 52

45-Degree Lunge 53

Front and Back Pulldown 54

Front Lunge 56

Front Raise 20

Front Squat to Push Press 57

Glute-Ham Raise 60

Hexagon Drill 99

Hip Press-Up 86

Hip Roll 88

Hip Rotation 89

Incline Press (Barbell) 62

Jump and Reach 100

Jump Over Barrier (Side) 101

Jump to Box 102

Knee Pull-In 90

Kneeling Side Throw 112

Lateral Cone Hops 103

Leg Curl (Facedown) 64

Leg Press 66

Overhead Throw 113

Pec Dec 68

Postworkout Stretches 28

Prone Fly 22

Pullover 70

Pullover and Press 72

Pullover Toss 114

Push Press 73

Push-Up With Clap 104

Russian Twist 92

Seated Row 74

Shoulder Stretch 1 25

Shoulder Stretch 2 26

Side Lateral Raise 18

Side Lunge 76

Side Sit-Up 94

Side-to-Side Box Shuffle 105

Single Leg Push-Off 106

Sit-Up With Legs Raised 96

Split Squat Jump 107

30-60-90 Box Drill 108

Upright Row 78

Walking Lunge 80

Wrist Flexion/Extension 81

Wrist/Forearm Stretch 27

Wrist Pronation/Supination 82

Wrist Ulnar/Radial Flexion 83

ABOUT THE AUTHOR

A frequent contributor to the *National Strength and Conditioning Association Journal,* Don Chu is a leading authority on power training and conditioning. In addition to serving as a consultant for the United States Tennis Association, Chu has been a conditioning consultant for the Golden State Warriors, Milwaukee Bucks, Detroit Lions, and Chicago White Sox. He is owner, director, and consultant to individual athletes at the Ather Sports Injury Clinic in northern California.

Dr. Chu earned his PhD in physical therapy and physical education from Stanford University and is a professor emeritus of kinesiology and physical education at California State University, Hayward. In 1978, his only year as a head coach, Dr. Chu was named the Far Western Conference Track and Field Coach of the Year. He is a registered physical therapist, a certified athletic trainer through the National Athletic Training Association, and a National Strength and Conditioning Association-certified strength specialist.

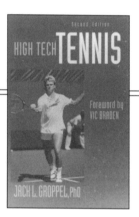

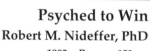

Training Videos from the USTA

Strength Training for Tennis
(36-minute videotape)

1993 • 1/2" VHS
Item MUST0389 • $24.95 ($33.50 Canadian)

Movement Training for Tennis
(35-minute videotape)

1990 • 1/2" VHS
Item MUST0392 • $24.95 ($33.50 Canadian)

Advanced Footskills for Tennis
(29-minute videotape)

1993 • 1/2" VHS
Item MUST0412 • $24.95 ($33.50 Canadian)

The Serve
(55-minute videotape)

Vic Braden Sports

1994 • 1/2" VHS • Item MBRA0413
$39.95 ($53.95 Canadian)

The Science and Myths of Tennis
(48-minute videotape)

Vic Braden and Howard Brody

1992 • 1/2" VHS • Item MBRA0378
$39.95 ($53.95 Canadian)

Women's Doubles
Made Easy the Vic Braden Way
(55-minute videotape)

Vic Braden

1992 • 1/2" VHS
Item MBRA0368
$39.95 ($53.95 Canadian)

Place your order using the appropriate
telephone number/address
shown in the front of this book,
or **call toll-free in U.S.(1-800-747-4457).**
Prices are subject to change.

Human Kinetics